MUSIC TELEVISION®

SELECTIONS FROM

100 greatest pop songs

Piano • Vocal • Guitar

W9-BRZ-530

There are some things you'll never forget: Your first kiss. Your first love. Your first heartbreak. And you will never ever forget the songs that were playing while all that was going on. Pop music is the soundtrack to our lives—the songs that are burned into our memories. To honor the best of them, MTV and Rolling Stone have compiled the 100 most creative, important, and timeless pop songs of the last four decades, from Beatlemania to boy band-mania, and all the hits in between. We're sure you'll have as much fun playing them as you did listening to them.

ISBN 0-634-05376-0

HAL•LEONARD®
CORPORATION
7777 W. BLUEMOUND RD. P.O. BOX 13819 MILWAUKEE, WI 53213

Visit Hal Leonard Online at
www.halleonard.com

100 greatest pop songs

RANK	SONG	ARTIST	YEAR
1.	Yesterday	*The Beatles*	1965
2.	(I Can't Get No) Satisfaction†	*The Rolling Stones*	1965
3.	Smells Like Teen Spirit	*Nirvana*	1991
4.	Like a Virgin	*Madonna*	1984
5.	Billie Jean	*Michael Jackson*	1983
6.	I Want to Hold Your Hand	*The Beatles*	1964
7.	Respect	*Aretha Franklin*	1967
8.	One	*U2*	1992
9.	I Want You Back	*The Jackson 5*	1969
10.	I Want It That Way	*Backstreet Boys*	1999
11.	Hotel California	*Eagles*	1977
12.	Where Did Our Love Go	*The Supremes*	1964
13.	Sweet Child o' Mine	*Guns N' Roses*	1988
14.	Brown Sugar†	*The Rolling Stones*	1971
15.	Imagine	*John Lennon with The Plastic Ono Band*	1971
16.	Nothing Compares 2 U†	*Sinead O'Connor*	1990
17.	Superstition	*Stevie Wonder*	1972
18.	Losing My Religion	*R.E.M.*	1991
19.	Vogue	*Madonna*	1990
20.	Like a Rolling Stone	*Bob Dylan*	1965
21.	Brown Eyed Girl	*Van Morrison*	1967
22.	Beat It	*Michael Jackson*	1983
23.	Oh, Pretty Woman	*Roy Orbison*	1964
24.	What's Going On	*Marvin Gaye*	1971
25.	…Baby One More Time	*Britney Spears*	1998
26.	Go Your Own Way	*Fleetwood Mac*	1977
27.	When Doves Cry†	*Prince*	1984
28.	In My Life	*The Beatles*	1965
29.	Bohemian Rhapsody	*Queen*	1975
30.	Your Song	*Elton John*	1970
31.	Smooth	*Santana featuring Rob Thomas*	1999
32.	(Sittin' On) The Dock of the Bay	*Otis Redding*	1968
33.	My Generation	*The Who*	1965
34.	You Oughta Know	*Alanis Morissette*	1995
35.	Born to Run†	*Bruce Springsteen*	1975
36.	Waterfalls	*TLC*	1995
37.	O.P.P.	*Naughty By Nature*	1991
38.	Changes	*David Bowie*	1972
39.	Iris	*Goo Goo Dolls*	1998
40.	I Will Always Love You	*Whitney Houston*	1992
41.	Proud Mary	*Creedence Clearwater Revival*	1969
42.	Every Breath You Take	*The Police*	1983
43.	Miss You	*The Rolling Stones*	1978
44.	Dancing Queen	*ABBA*	1976
45.	Tears in Heaven	*Eric Clapton*	1992
46.	The Tracks of My Tears	*The Miracles*	1965

RANK	SONG	ARTIST	YEAR
47.	Jump	*Van Halen*	1984
48.	Jeremy†	*Pearl Jam*	1992
49.	Tangled Up in Blue	*Bob Dylan*	1975
50.	Little Red Corvette†	*Prince*	1983
51.	Just My Imagination (Running Away with Me)	*The Temptations*	1971
52.	Maybe I'm Amazed	*Paul McCartney*	1970
53.	Faith	*George Michael*	1987
54.	Under the Bridge	*Red Hot Chili Peppers*	1992
55.	Bye Bye Bye	**NSYNC*	2000
56.	I Will Survive	*Gloria Gaynor*	1979
57.	Our Lips Are Sealed	*Go-Go's*	1981
58.	One Headlight	*The Wallflowers*	1997
59.	You Are the Sunshine of My Life	*Stevie Wonder*	1973
60.	Just the Way You Are	*Billy Joel*	1977
61.	The One I Love	*R.E.M.*	1987
62.	Papa Don't Preach	*Madonna*	1986
63.	MMM Bop	*Hanson*	1997
64.	Bennie and the Jets	*Elton John*	1974
65.	Just What I Needed	*The Cars*	1978
66.	Time After Time	*Cyndi Lauper*	1984
67.	My Name Is	*Eminem*	1999
68.	Only Happy When It Rains	*Garbage*	1996
69.	Just Can't Get Enough	*Depeche Mode*	1981
70.	Good Vibrations	*The Beach Boys*	1966
71.	I Wanna Be Sedated	*The Ramones*	1979
72.	Free Fallin'	*Tom Petty*	1989
73.	Do You Really Want to Hurt Me	*Culture Club*	1982
74.	Tiny Dancer	*Elton John*	1972
75.	Hot Fun in the Summertime	*Sly & The Family Stone*	1969
76.	Creep	*Radiohead*	1993
77.	Let's Stay Together	*Al Green*	1971
78.	Longview	*Green Day*	1994
79.	Nasty	*Janet Jackson*	1986
80.	I Need Love	*LL Cool J*	1987
81.	Don't Speak	*No Doubt*	1996
82.	Rock with You	*Michael Jackson*	1979
83.	I Want to Know What Love Is	*Foreigner*	1984
84.	Wonderwall	*Oasis*	1995
85.	Surrender	*Cheap Trick*	1978
86.	Don't You Want Me	*The Human League*	1982
87.	Brass in Pocket	*The Pretenders*	1980
88.	Gone till November	*Wyclef Jean*	1998
89.	Careless Whisper	*Wham! featuring George Michael*	1984
90.	The Boy Is Mine	*Brandy & Monica*	1998
91.	No Diggity	*Blackstreet*	1996
92.	You Shook Me All Night Long	*AC/DC*	1980
93.	Stayin' Alive	*Bee Gees*	1977
94.	All the Small Things	*Blink 182*	1999
95.	Good Times	*Chic*	1979
96.	Photograph	*Def Leppard*	1983
97.	Love Shack	*The B-52's*	1989
98.	She Drives Me Crazy	*Fine Young Cannibals*	1989
99.	Just a Friend	*Biz Markie*	1989
100.	Tainted Love	*Soft Cell*	1982

†Omitted from this publication because of licensing restrictions.

contents

6	All the Small Things	Blink 182
12	...Baby One More Time	Britney Spears
16	Beat It	Michael Jackson
28	Bennie and the Jets	Elton John
32	Billie Jean	Michael Jackson
36	Bohemian Rhapsody	Queen
21	The Boy Is Mine	Brandy & Monica
46	Brass in Pocket	The Pretenders
50	Brown Eyed Girl	Van Morrison
56	Bye Bye Bye	*NSYNC
53	Careless Whisper	Wham! featuring George Michael
60	Changes	David Bowie
66	Creep	Radiohead
71	Dancing Queen	ABBA
74	Do You Really Want to Hurt Me	Culture Club
81	(Sittin' On) The Dock of the Bay	Otis Redding
84	Don't Speak	No Doubt
96	Don't You Want Me	The Human League
89	Every Breath You Take	The Police
100	Faith	George Michael
104	Free Fallin'	Tom Petty
108	Go Your Own Way	Fleetwood Mac
112	Gone till November	Wyclef Jean
118	Good Times	Chic
122	Good Vibrations	The Beach Boys
131	Hot Fun in the Summertime	Sly & The Family Stone
136	Hotel California	Eagles
148	I Need Love	LL Cool J
143	I Wanna Be Sedated	The Ramones
152	I Want It That Way	Backstreet Boys
156	I Want to Hold Your Hand	The Beatles
160	I Want to Know What Love Is	Foreigner
164	I Want You Back	The Jackson 5
168	I Will Always Love You	Whitney Houston
173	I Will Survive	Gloria Gaynor
178	Imagine	John Lennon with The Plastic Ono Band
182	In My Life	The Beatles
190	Iris	Goo Goo Dolls
200	Jump	Van Halen
208	Just a Friend	Biz Markie
210	Just Can't Get Enough	Depeche Mode
185	Just My Imagination (Running Away with Me)	The Temptations
214	Just the Way You Are	Billy Joel
228	Just What I Needed	The Cars
232	Let's Stay Together	Al Green
223	Like a Rolling Stone	Bob Dylan
236	Like a Virgin	Madonna

240	**Longview**	Green Day
248	**Losing My Religion**	R.E.M.
254	**Love Shack**	The B-52's
245	**Maybe I'm Amazed**	Paul McCartney
260	**Miss You**	The Rolling Stones
267	**MMM Bop**	Hanson
274	**My Generation**	The Who
284	**My Name Is**	Eminem
277	**Nasty**	Janet Jackson
288	**No Diggity**	Blackstreet
297	**O.P.P.**	Naughty By Nature
302	**Oh, Pretty Woman**	Roy Orbison
309	**One**	U2
316	**One Headlight**	The Wallflowers
322	**The One I Love**	R.E.M.
326	**Only Happy When It Rains**	Garbage
338	**Our Lips Are Sealed**	Go-Go's
331	**Papa Don't Preach**	Madonna
342	**Photograph**	Def Leppard
348	**Proud Mary**	Creedence Clearwater Revival
353	**Respect**	Aretha Franklin
358	**Rock with You**	Michael Jackson
366	**She Drives Me Crazy**	Fine Young Cannibals
370	**Smells Like Teen Spirit**	Nirvana
375	**Smooth**	Santana featuring Rob Thomas
382	**Stayin' Alive**	Bee Gees
387	**Superstition**	Stevie Wonder
392	**Surrender**	Cheap Trick
398	**Sweet Child o' Mine**	Guns N' Roses
405	**Tainted Love**	Soft Cell
410	**Tangled Up in Blue**	Bob Dylan
414	**Tears in Heaven**	Eric Clapton
424	**Time After Time**	Cyndi Lauper
428	**Tiny Dancer**	Elton John
434	**The Tracks of My Tears**	The Miracles
419	**Under the Bridge**	Red Hot Chili Peppers
438	**Vogue**	Madonna
448	**Waterfalls**	TLC
454	**What's Going On**	Marvin Gaye
460	**Where Did Our Love Go**	The Supremes
465	**Wonderwall**	Oasis
470	**Yesterday**	The Beatles
473	**You Are the Sunshine of My Life**	Stevie Wonder
476	**You Oughta Know**	Alanis Morissette
481	**You Shook Me All Night Long**	AC/DC
488	**Your Song**	Elton John

ALL THE SMALL THINGS

Words and Music by TOM DeLONGE
and MARK HOPPUS

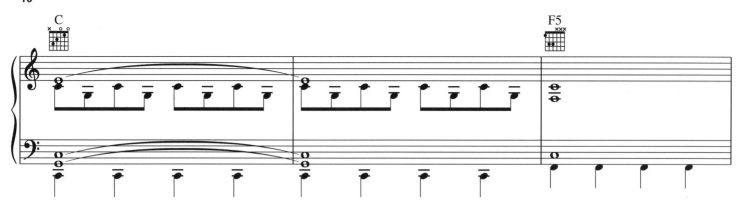

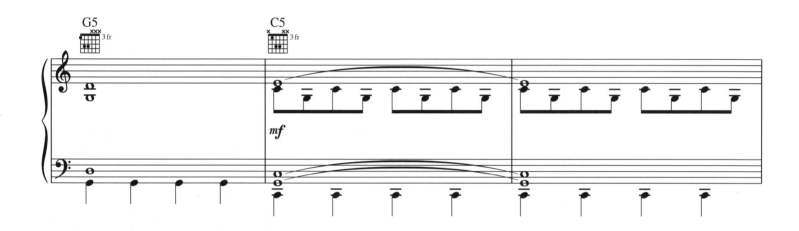

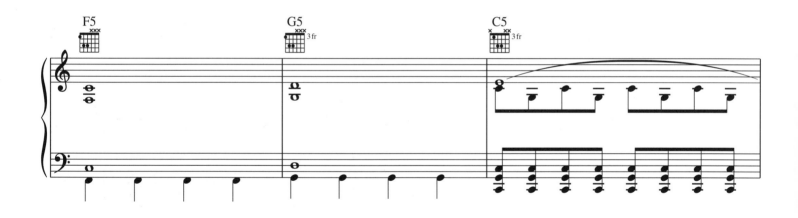

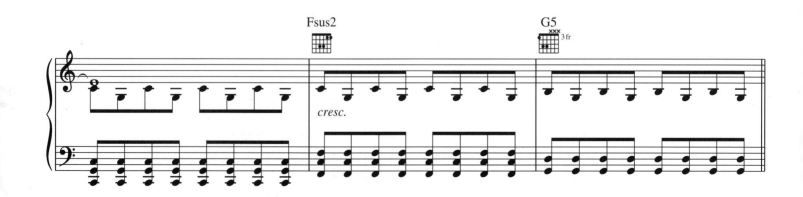

...BABY ONE MORE TIME

Words and Music by
MAX MARTIN

Oh, ba-by, ba-by.   Oh, ba-by, ba-by.

Oh, ba-by, ba-by, how was I sup-posed to know that
Oh, ba-by, ba-by, the rea-son I breathe is you.

some-thing was-n't right here?   Oh, ba-by, ba-by,   I should-n't have let you go.
Boy, you've got me blind-ed.   Oh, pret-ty ba-by, there's noth-ing that I would-n't

BEAT IT

Written and Composed by
MICHAEL JACKSON

Original key: Eb minor. This edition has been transposed up one half-step to be more playable.

THE BOY IS MINE

Words and Music by LaSHAWN DANIELS,
JAPHE TEJEDA, RODNEY JERKINS,
FRED JERKINS and BRANDY NORWOOD

Brandy: Excuse me, can I please talk to you for a minute?   *Monica: Uh huh, sure. You know,*

you look kind of familiar. Brandy: Yeah, you do too. But, um, I just wanted to know, do you know

BENNIE AND THE JETS

Words and Music by ELTON JOHN
and BERNIE TAUPIN

Slowly, deliberately

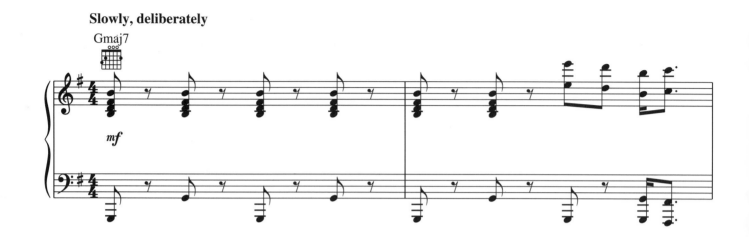

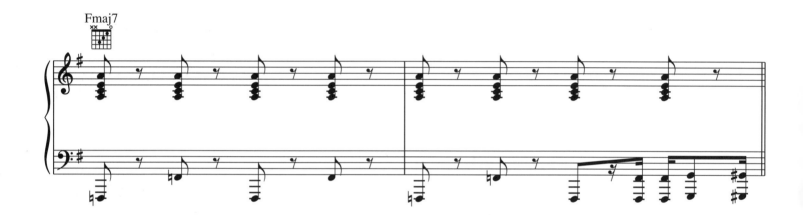

Hey, kids,__ shake__ it loose to-geth - er. The spot - light's hit-ting some-thing that's been known to change the weath-er.
Hey, kids,__ plug __ in-to the faith-less. May - be they're__ blind-ed, but Ben - nie makes them age-less.
Solo ad lib.

BILLIE JEAN

Written and Composed by
MICHAEL JACKSON

BOHEMIAN RHAPSODY

Words and Music by
FREDDIE MERCURY

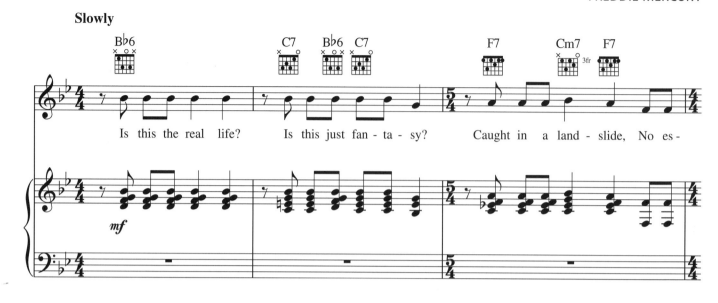

BRASS IN POCKET

Words and Music by CHRISSIE HYNDE
and JAMES HONEYMAN-SCOTT

Moderate Rock

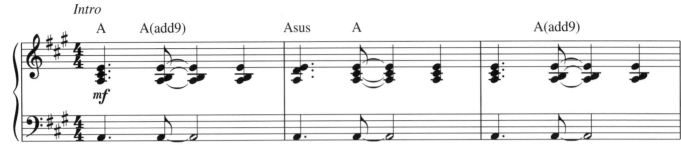

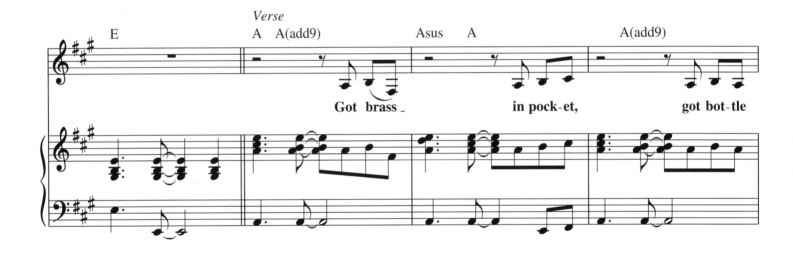

BROWN EYED GIRL

Words and Music by
VAN MORRISON

Additional Lyrics

2. Whatever happened to Tuesday and so slow
   Going down the old mine with a transistor radio
   Standing in the sunlight laughing
   Hiding behind a rainbow's wall
   Slipping and a-sliding
   All along the water fall
   With you, my brown eyed girl
   You, my brown eyed girl.
   Do you remember when we used to sing:
   Chorus

3. So hard to find my way, now that I'm all on my own
   I saw you just the other day, my, how you have grown
   Cast my memory back there, Lord
   Sometime I'm overcome thinking 'bout
   Making love in the green grass
   Behind the stadium
   With you, my brown eyed girl
   With you, my brown eyed girl.
   Do you remember when we used to sing:
   Chorus

CARELESS WHISPER

Words and Music by GEORGE MICHAEL
and ANDREW RIDGELEY

BYE BYE BYE

Words and Music by KRISTIAN LUNDIN,
JAKE CARLSSON and ANDREAS CARLSSON

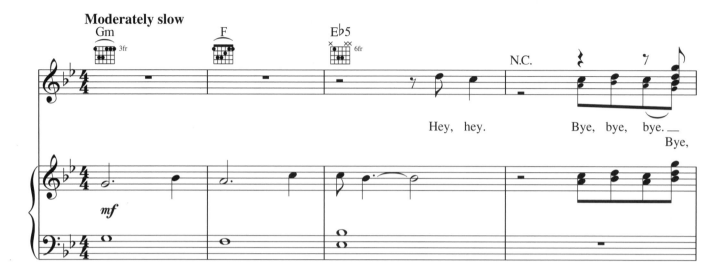

Original key: G♯ minor. This edition has been transposed down one half-step to be more playable.

CHANGES

Words and Music by
DAVID BOWIE

1. I still don't know what I ____ was
2. *(See additional lyrics)*

wait-ing for and my time was run-ning wild. A mil-lion dead - end streets, _ and

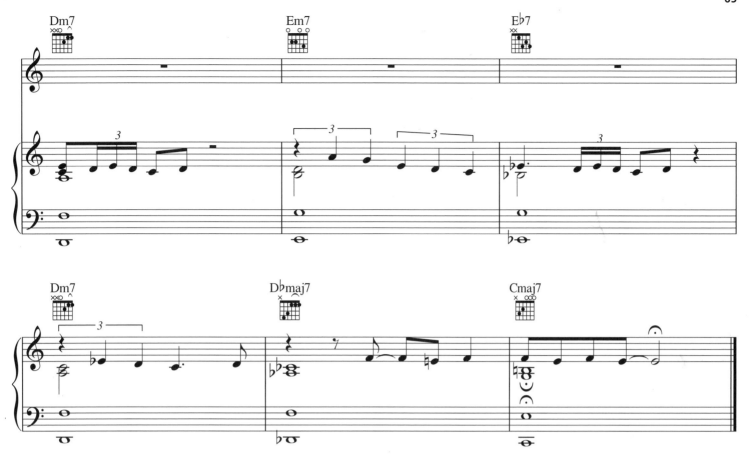

Additional Lyrics

2. I watch the ripples change their size, but never leave the stream
   Of warm impermanence and so the days flowed through my eyes
   But still the days seem the same.
   And these children that you spit on as they try to change their worlds
   Are immune to your consultations, they're quite aware of what they're going through.

   (Ch-ch-ch-ch-Changes) Turn and face the strange.
   (Ch-ch-changes) Don't tell them to grow up and out of it.
   (Ch-ch-ch-ch-Changes) Turn and face the strange.
   (Ch-ch-changes) Where's your shame? You've left us up to our necks in it.
   Time may change me, but you can't trace time.

CREEP

Words and Music by ALBERT HAMMOND,
MIKE HAZLEWOOD, THOMAS YORKE,
RICHARD GREENWOOD, PHILIP SELWAY,
COLIN GREENWOOD and EDWARD O'BRIAN

you're so fuck-in' spe - cial.
I wish I were spe - cial.
I wish I were spe - cial.

But I'm a creep, ___

I'm a weird - o. ___

What the hell ___ am I do-ing here? ___

DANCING QUEEN

Words and Music by BENNY ANDERSSON,
BJORN ULVAEUS and STIG ANDERSON

DO YOU REALLY WANT TO HURT ME

Words and Music by GEORGE O'DOWD, JON MOSS,
MICHAEL CRAIG and ROY HAY

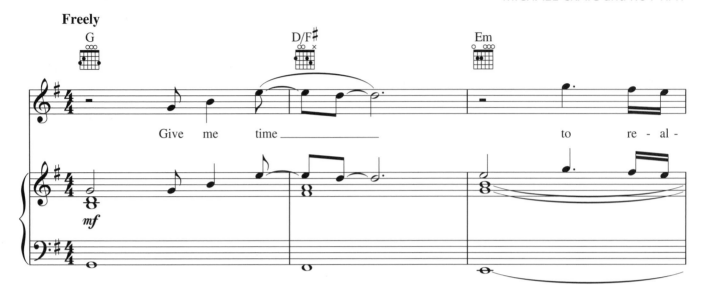

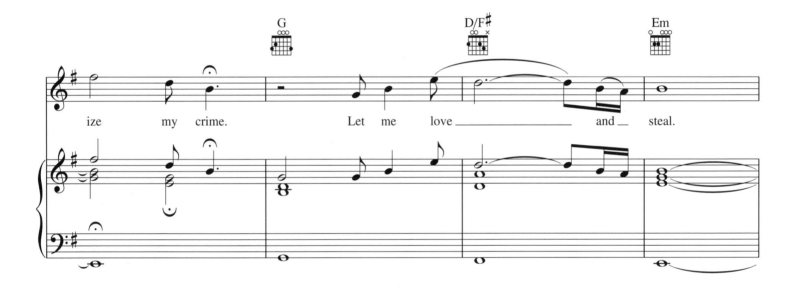

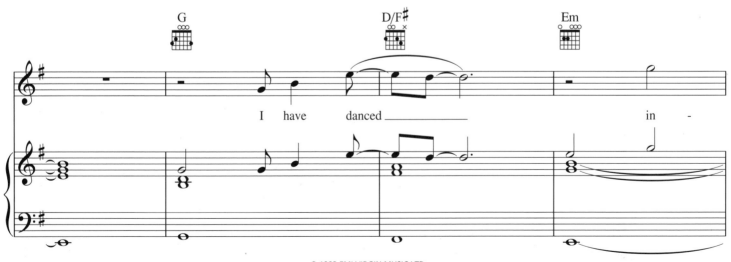

Do you real-ly want to hurt me? __ Do you real-ly want to

make me cry? _____

To Coda ⊕

Words are few __ I __ have spok - en.
You've been talk-in', but __ be - lieve me.

I could waste a thou - sand
If it's true you do __ not

Do you real-ly want to make me cry? _____

Do you real-ly want to hurt me? _____

Do you real-ly want to make me cry? _____

(Sittin' On)
THE DOCK OF THE BAY

Words and Music by STEVE CROPPER
and OTIS REDDING

Moderate beat

Sit - tin' in the morn - ing sun, _____ I'll be
left my _____ home _____ in Geor - gia
Sit - tin' here _____ rest - in' my bones, _____ and this

sit - tin' when the eve - nin' _____ come. _____
head - ed for the Fris - co _____ bay. _____
lone - li - ness won't leave my a - lone. _____

Watch - in' the ships roll in, _____ then I
I have _____ noth - in' to live _____ for, look like
Two thou - sand miles I roam _____ just to

DON'T SPEAK

Words and Music by ERIC STEFANI
and GWEN STEFANI

You and me, we used to be to-geth - er, ev-'ry day to-geth - er, al -

- ways. I real-ly feel _____ that I'm los - ing my best friend. I

can't be-lieve this could be the ____ end. It looks as though ____ you're
As we die, ____ both ____

EVERY BREATH YOU TAKE

Music and Lyrics by
STING

Moderate Rock

long for your em-brace. I keep cry - ing, ba - by, ba - by, please

DON'T YOU WANT ME

Words and Music by PHIL OAKEY,
ADRIAN WRIGHT and JO CALLIS

Additional Lyrics

3. I was working as a waitress in a cocktail bar,
   That much is true.
   But even then I knew I'd find a much better place
   Either with or without you.

4. The five years we have had have been such good times,
   I still love you.
   But now I think it's time I live my life on my own.
   I guess it's just what I must do.

FAITH

Words and Music by
GEORGE MICHAEL

Brightly, with a beat

Well, I guess it would be

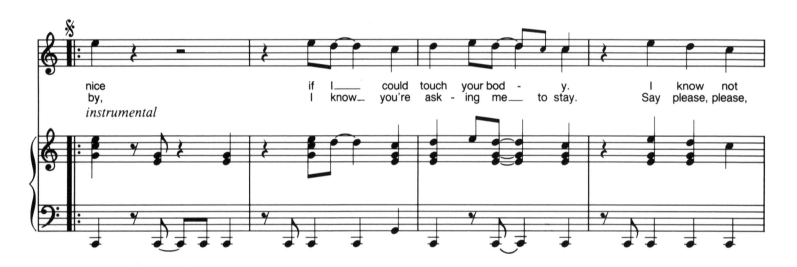

nice
by,   if I____ could touch your bod - - y.   I know not
instrumental   I know____ you're ask - ing me____ to stay.   Say please, please,

ev - 'ry - bod - - - - y   has got a bod - y like   you.____   Oh,   but I got - ta think
please don't go____ a - way.   You say I'm giv - ing you the   blues.____   May   - be

FREE FALLIN'

Words and Music by TOM PETTY
and JEFF LYNNE

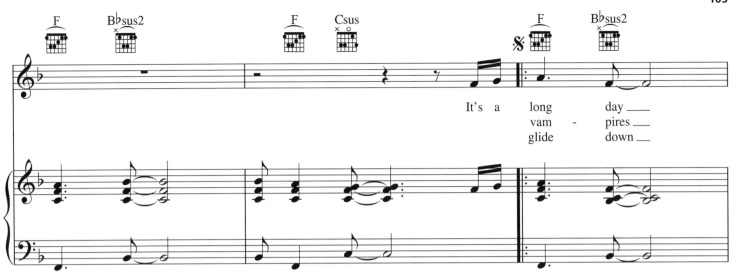

It's a long day ___
vam - pires ___
glide down ___

liv - in' in Re - se - da. There's a free - way ___ run - nin' through the yard. ___ And I'm a
walk - in' through the val - ley move ___ west down ___ Ven - tur - a Boul - e - vard. And all the
o - ver Mul - hol - land. I wan - na write her ___ name in the sky. ___ I wan - na

bad boy ___ 'cause I don't e - ven miss ___ her. I'm a bad boy ___ for
bad boys ___ are stand - ing in the shad - ows. And the good girls ___ are
free fall ___ out in - to noth - in'. Gon - na leave this ___

GO YOUR OWN WAY

Words and Music by
LINDSEY BUCKINGHAM

Lov - ing you
Tell __ me why
Instrumental

is - n't the right _____ thing __ to do.
ev - 'ry - thing turned _____ a - round.

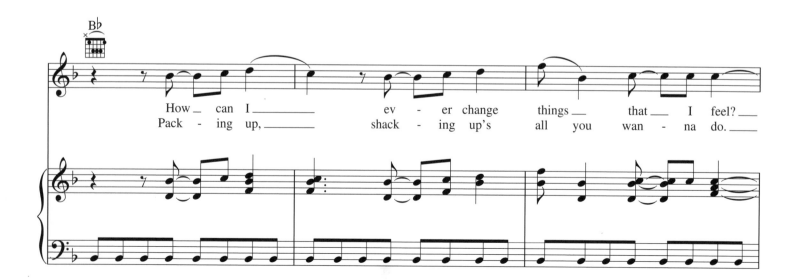

How __ can I _____ ev - er change things __ that __ I feel?
Pack - ing up, _____ shack - ing up's all you wan - na do. _____

GONE TILL NOVEMBER

Words and Music by
WYCLEF JEAN

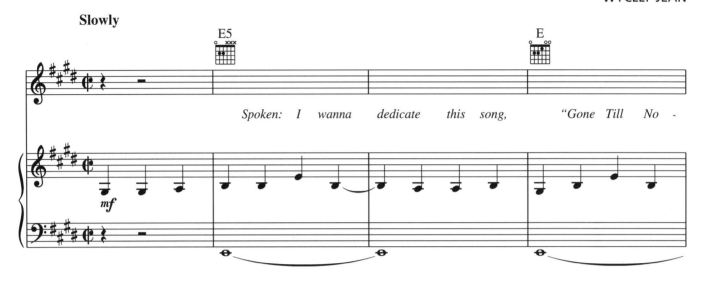

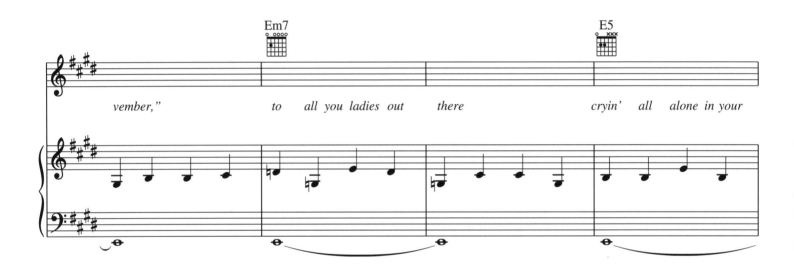

south ____ not makin' it back, may the Lord bless your soul. I love you, girl.

Sung: Ev-'ry-time ____ I make __ a run, ____ girl, you turn __

____ a-round __ and cry. _____ I ____ ask my-self

why, oh why. _____ See, you __

GOOD TIMES

Words and Music by NILE RODGERS
and BERNARD EDWARDS

GOOD VIBRATIONS

Words and Music by BRIAN WILSON
and MIKE LOVE

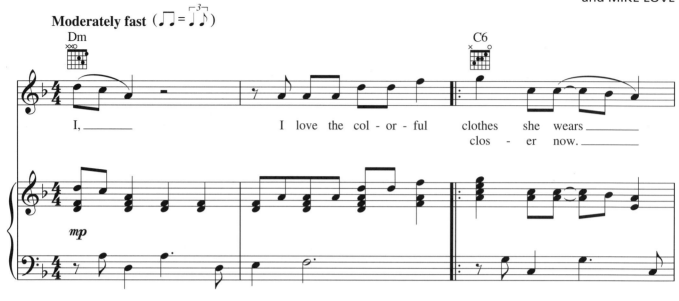

I, _____
I love the col-or-ful clothes she wears _____
clos - er now. _____

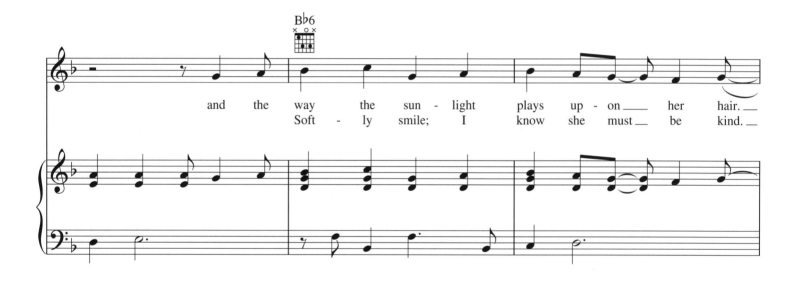

and the way the sun - light plays up - on ____ her hair. ___
Soft - ly smile; I know she must ___ be kind. ___

I _____
When _____

Original key: E♭ minor. This edition has been transposed down one half-step to be more playable.

HOT FUN IN THE SUMMERTIME

Words and Music by
SYLVESTER STEWART

HOTEL CALIFORNIA

Words and Music by DON HENLEY,
GLENN FREY and DON FELDER

I saw a shim-mer-ing light.
sweet ___ sum-mer sweat.

My head grew heav-y and my
Some ___ dance ___ to re-

sight grew dim; ___
mem - ber; ___

I had to stop for the night. ___
some ___ dance to for-get. ___

There she stood in the door-way;
So I called up the cap - tain:

I heard the mis-sion bell. ___
"Please bring me my

___ wine." He said,

And I was think-ing to my-self: ___ this could be
"We have-n't had that spir-it here ___ since ___

I WANNA BE SEDATED

Words and Music by JEFFREY HYMAN,
JOHN CUMMINGS and DOUGLAS COLVIN

I NEED LOVE

Words and Music by JAMES TODD SMITH,
DWAYNE SIMON, BOBBY ERVING,
DARRYL PIERCE and STEVEN ETTINGER

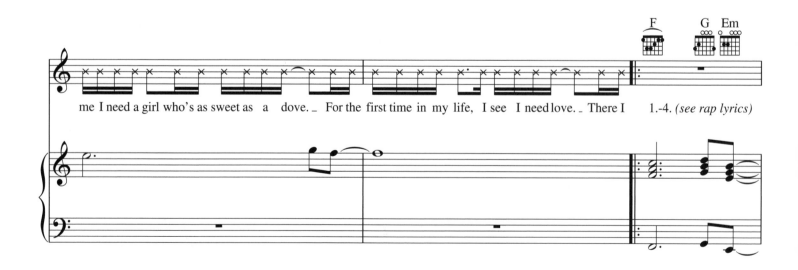

Spoken: Girl, listen to me.

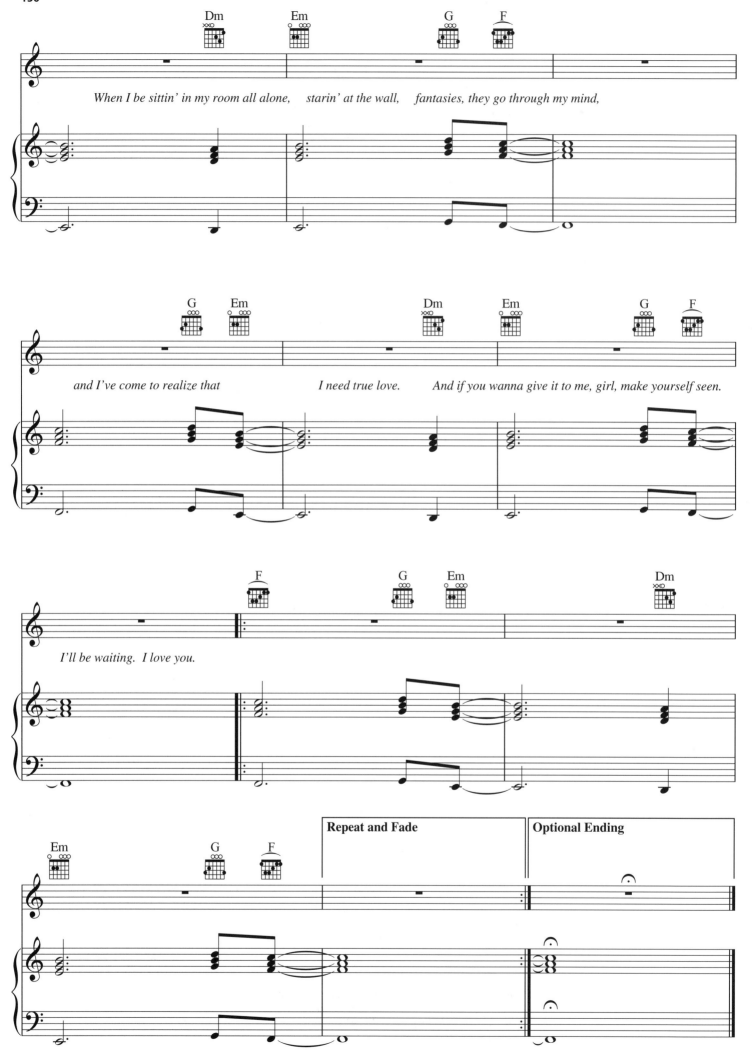

Rap Lyrics

1. There I was, giggling about the games
   That I had played with many hearts, and I'm not sayin' no more names.
   Then the thought occured, teardrops made my eyes burn
   As I said to myself, "Look what you've done to her."
   I can feel it inside; I can't explain how it feels,
   All I know is that I'll never dish another raw deal,
   Playin' make-believe, pretending that I'm true,
   Holding in my laugh as I say that I love you.
   Saying, "Amor," kissing you on the ear,
   Whispering, "I love you" and, "I'll always be here."
   Although I often reminisce, I can't believe that I found
   A desire for true love floatin' around
   Inside my soul. Because my soul is cold,
   One half of me deserves to be this way till I'm old.
   But the other half needs affection and joy,
   And the warmth that is created by a girl and a boy.
   I need love. I need love.

2. Romance, sheer delight, how sweet!
   I gotta find me a girl to make my life complete.
   You could scratch my back; we'll get cozy and huddle.
   I'll lay down my jacket so you can walk over a puddle.
   I'd give you a rose, pull out your chair before we eat,
   Kiss you on the cheek and say, "Ooh, girl, you're so sweet."
   It's deja vu whenever I'm with you;
   I could go on forever tellin' you what I'd do.
   But where you at? You're neither here nor there.
   I swear I can't find you anywhere.
   Damn sure ain't in my closet, or under my rug.
   This love search is really makin' me bug.
   And if you know who you are, why don't you make yourself seen?
   Take a chance with my love, and you'll find out what I mean.
   Fantasies can run, but they can't hide.
   And when I find you, I'm gonna pour all my love inside.
   I need love. I need love.

3. I wanna kiss you, hold you, never scold you, just love you,
   Suck on your neck, caress you and rub you,
   Grind, moan, and never be alone.
   If you're not standin' next to me, you're on the phone.
   Can't you hear it in my voice? I need love bad.
   I got money, but love's somethin' I've never had.
   I need your ruby red lips, sweet face and all.
   I love you more than a man who's ten feet tall.
   I watch the sun rise in your eyes.
   We're so in love, when we hug, we become paralyzed.
   Our bodies explode in ecstasy unreal.
   You're as soft as a pillow and I'm hard as steel.
   It's like a dreamland; I can't lie, I never been there.
   Maybe this is an experience that me and you can share.
   Clean and unsoiled, yet sweaty and wet.
   I swear to you, this is somethin' I'll never forget.
   I need love. I need love.

4. See what I mean? I've changed; I'm no longer
   A playboy on the run, I need somethin' that's stronger.
   Friendship, trust, honor, respect, admiration;
   This whole experience has been such a revelation.
   It's taught me love and how to be a real man,
   To always be considerate and do all I can,
   Protect you; you're my lady and you mean so much.
   My body tingles all over from the slightest touch
   Of your hand, and understand, I'll be frozen in time
   Till we meet face to face and you tell me your mind.
   If I find you, girl, I swear I'll be a good man;
   I'm not gonna leave it in destiny's hands.
   I can't sit and wait for my princess to arrive;
   I've gotta struggle and fight to keep my dream alive.
   I'll search the whole world for that special girl;
   When I finally find you, watch our love unfurl.
   I need love. I need love.

I WANT IT THAT WAY

Words and Music by MAX MARTIN
and ANDREAS CARLSSON

I WANT TO HOLD YOUR HAND

Words and Music by JOHN LENNON
and PAUL McCARTNEY

Oh yeah,

I'll _____ tell you some - thing
please _____ say to me _____

I think you'll un - der -
you'll let me be your

stand.
man,

When I _____ say that some - thing,
and please _____ say to me _____

I WANT TO KNOW WHAT LOVE IS

Words and Music by
MICK JONES

I WANT YOU BACK

Words and Music by FREDDIE PERREN,
ALPHONSO MIZELL, BERRY GORDY and DEKE RICHARDS

I WILL ALWAYS LOVE YOU

Words and Music by
DOLLY PARTON

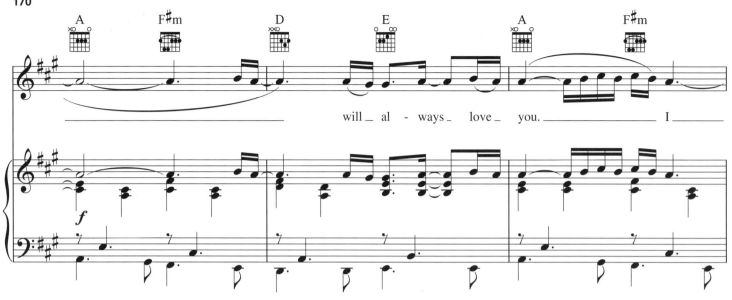

will _ al - ways _ love _ you. _____ I

D.S.

___ will _ al - ways _ love _ you. _____

CODA

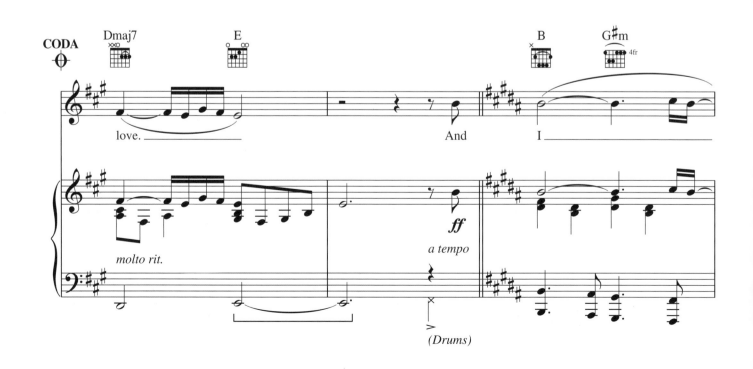

love. _____ And I _____

molto rit.

a tempo

ff

(Drums)

Additional Lyrics

3. I hope life treats you kind.
   And I hope you have all you've dreamed of.
   And I wish to you, joy and happiness.
   But above all this, I wish you love.

I WILL SURVIVE

Words and Music by DINO FEKARIS
and FREDERICK J. PERREN

IMAGINE

Words and Music by
JOHN LENNON

IN MY LIFE

Words and Music by JOHN LENNON
and PAUL McCARTNEY

JUST MY IMAGINATION
(Running Away with Me)

Words and Music by NORMAN J. WHITFIELD
and BARRETT STRONG

IRIS

Words and Music by
JOHN RZEZNIK

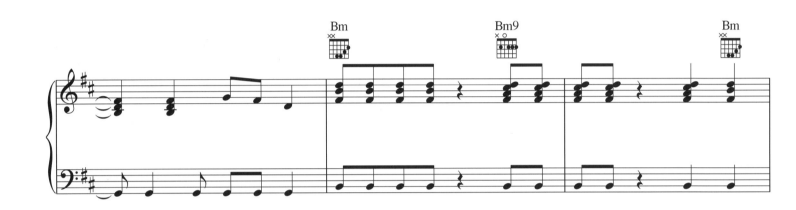

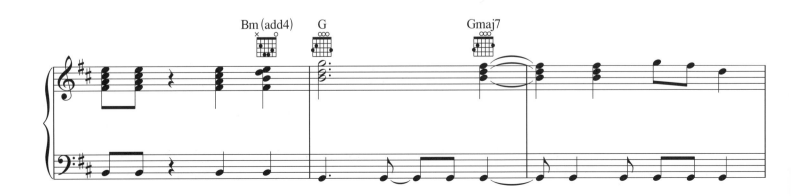

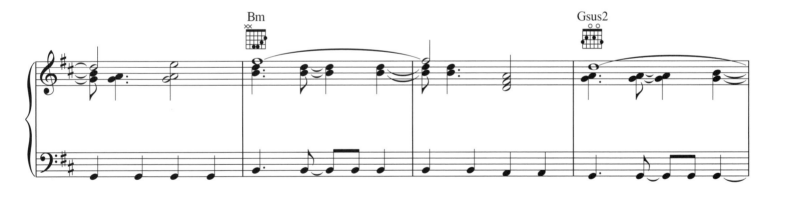

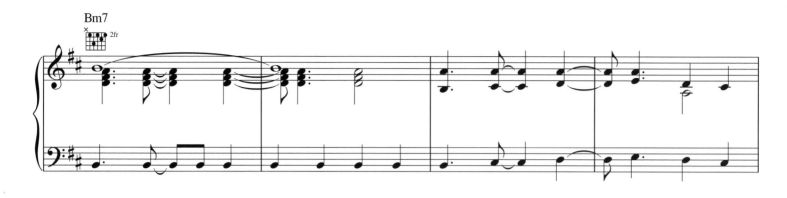

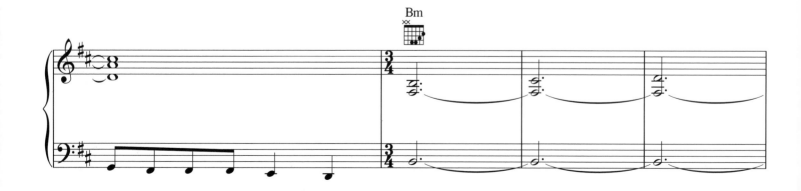

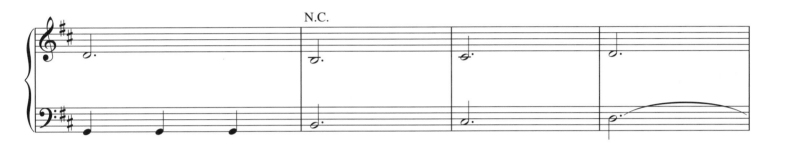

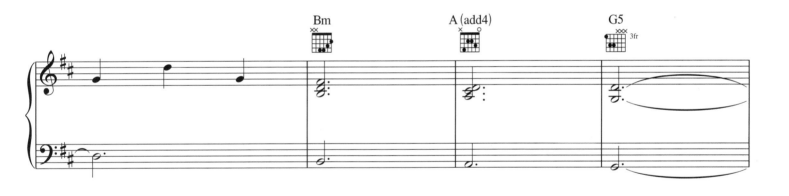

And I ___ don't want the world ___ to see ___ me

JUMP

Words and Music by EDWARD VAN HALEN, ALEX VAN HALEN,
MICHAEL ANTHONY and DAVID LEE ROTH

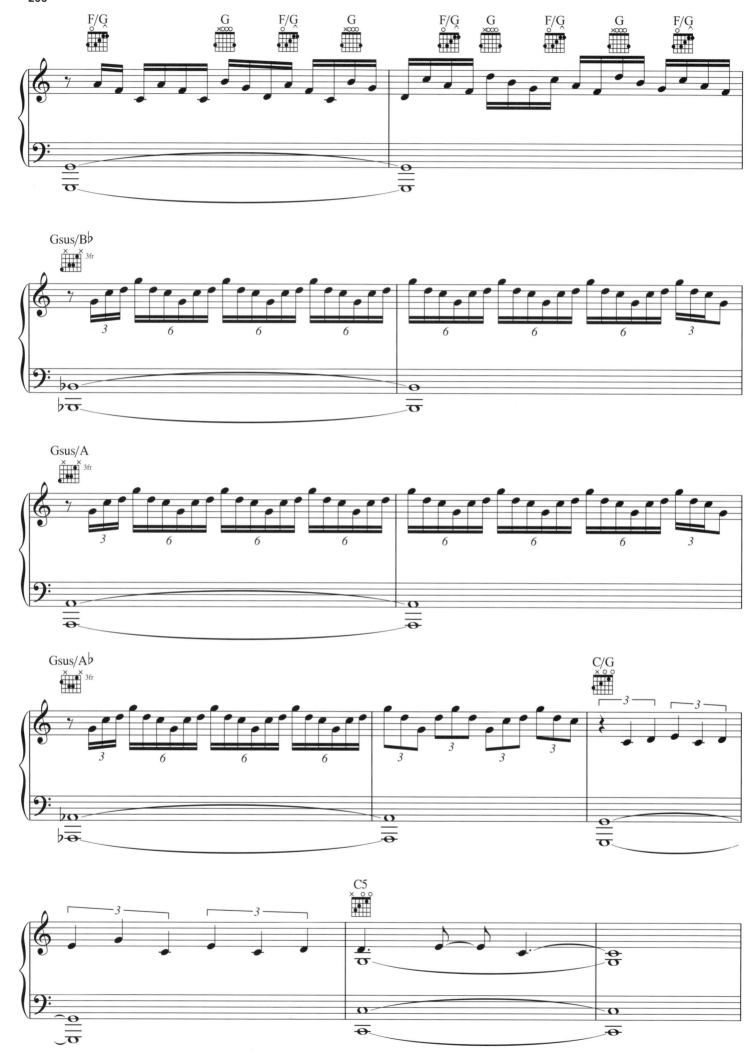

JUST A FRIEND

Words and Music by
BIZ MARKIE

Rap Lyrics

1. Have you ever met a girl that you tried to date,
   But a year to make love she wanted you to wait?
   Let me tell ya a story of my situation.
   I was talkin' to this girl from the U.S. nation.
   The way that I met her was on tour at a concert.
   She had long hair and a short miniskirt.
   I just got offstage, drippin', pourin' with sweat,
   I was walkin' through the crowd and guess who I met.
   I whispered in her ear, "Come to the picture booth,
   So I can ask you some questions to see if you're hundred proof."
   I asked her her name, she said blah-blah-blah.
   She had 9/10 pants and a very big bra.
   I took a couple of flicks and she was enthused.
   I said, "How do you like the show?"
   She said, "I was very amused."
   I started throwin' bass, she started throwin' back mid-range.
   But when I sprung the question, she acted kind of strange.
   Then when I asked, "Do ya have a man?" she tried to pretend.
   She said, "No, I don't, I only have a friend,"
   Come on, I'm not even goin' for it,
   This is what I'm gonna sing:
   Chorus

2. So I took blah-blah's word for it at this time.
   I thought just havin' a friend couldn't be no crime.
   'Cause I have friends and that's a fact,
   Like Agnes, Agatha, Germaine, and Jack.
   Forget about that, let's go into the story
   About a girl named blah-blah-blah that adore me.
   So we started talkin', gettin' familiar,
   Spendin' a lot of time so we can build
   A relationship or some understanding
   How it's gonna be in the future we was plannin'.
   Everything sounded so dandy and sweet,
   I had no idea I was in for a treat.
   After this was established, everything was cool.
   The tour was over and she went back to school.
   I called every day to see how she was doin'.
   Every time that I called her, it seemed somethin' was brewin'.
   I called her room, a guy picked up, and then I called again.
   I said, "Yo, who was that?" "Oh, he's just a friend."
   Don't gimme that, don't even gimme that.
   Jus' bust this:
   Chorus

3. So I came to her college on a surprise visit,
   To see my girl that was so exquisite.
   It was a school day, I knew she was there,
   The first semester of the school year.
   I went to a gate to ask where was her dorm,
   This guy made me fill out a visitor's form.
   He told me where it was, and I was on my way
   To see my baby doll, I was happy to say.
   I arrived in front of the dormitory.
   "Yo, could you tell me where is door three?"
   They showed me where it was. For the moment
   I didn't know I was in for such an event.
   So I came to her room and opened the door.
   Oh, snap! Guess what I saw!
   A fella tongue-kissin' my girl in the mouth.
   I was so in shock my heart went down south.
   So please listen to the message that I send:
   Don't ever talk to a girl who says she just has a friend.

JUST CAN'T GET ENOUGH

Words and Music by
VINCE CLARK

When I'm with you, ba - by, I go out_ of my head, and I just can't get e - nough, and I
We walk to - geth - er, we're walk - ing_ down_ the street, and I just can't get e - nough, and I
And when it rains, __ you're shin - ing_ down_ for me, and I just can't get e - nough,

just can't get e-nough. All the things you do to me and ev-'ry-thing you said, I
just can't get e-nough. Ev-'ry time I think of you, I know we have to meet, and I
just can't get e-nough. Just like a rain-bow, you know you set me free, and I

just can't get e-nough, and I just can't get e-nough. We slip and slide as we
just can't get e-nough, and I just can't get e-nough. It's get-ting hot-ter, it's our
just can't get e-nough, and I just can't get e-nough. You're like an an-gel and you

fall in love, and I just can't seem to get e-nough, ah!
burn-ing love, and I just can't seem to get e-nough, ah!
give me your love, and I just can't seem to get e-nough, ah!

JUST THE WAY YOU ARE

Words and Music by
BILLY JOEL

LIKE A ROLLING STONE

Words and Music by
BOB DYLAN

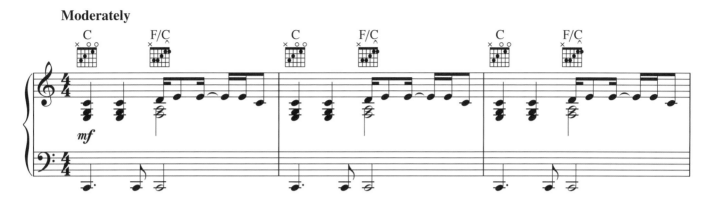

1. Once up-on __ a time you dressed so fine, __
2. __ gone __ to the fin-est school, __ al-
3. __ nev-er turned __ a-round to see the frowns
4. (See additional lyrics)

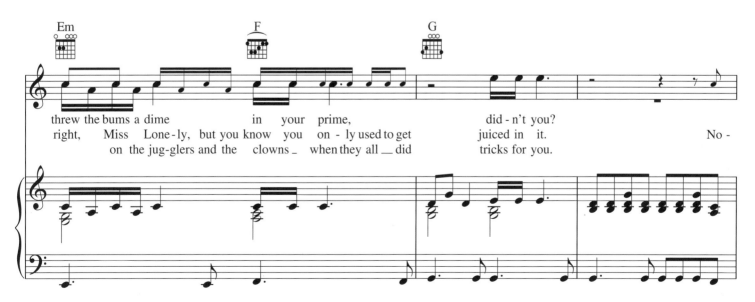

threw the bums a dime __ in your prime, __ did-n't you?
right, Miss Lone-ly, but you know you on-ly used to get juiced in it. No-
on the jug-glers and the clowns __ when they all __ did tricks for you.

Peo-ple call, say, "Be - ware, doll, you're bound to fall." You thought they were all
bod-y's ev - er taught you how to live out on the street and now you're gon - na have to get
Nev - er un - der-stood that it ain't no good you should - n't let oth - er peo - ple get your

a - kid -din' you.
used to it.
kicks for you.

You used to
You say you
You used to ride on a chrome horse with your

laugh a - bout ev' - ry - bod - y that was hang - in' out.
nev - er com - pro - mise with the mys - ter - y tramp, but now you re - al - ize
dip - lo - mat who car - ried on his shoul - der a Sia - mese cat.

Additional Lyrics

4. Princess on the steeple and all the pretty people
They're all drinkin', thinkin' that they got it made.
Exchanging all precious gifts,
But you better take your diamond ring,
You'd better pawn it, babe.
You used to be so amused
At Napoleon in rags and the language that he used.
Go to him now, he calls you, you can't refuse.
When you got nothin', you got nothin' to lose.
You're invisible now, you got no secrets to conceal.
Chorus

JUST WHAT I NEEDED

Words and Music by
RIC OCASEK

LET'S STAY TOGETHER

Words and Music by AL GREEN,
WILLIE MITCHELL and AL JACKSON, JR.

LIKE A VIRGIN

Words and Music by BILLY STEINBERG
and TOM KELLY

LONGVIEW

Words by BILLIE JOE
Music by BILLIE JOE,
TRE COOL and MIKE DIRNT

Moderately fast

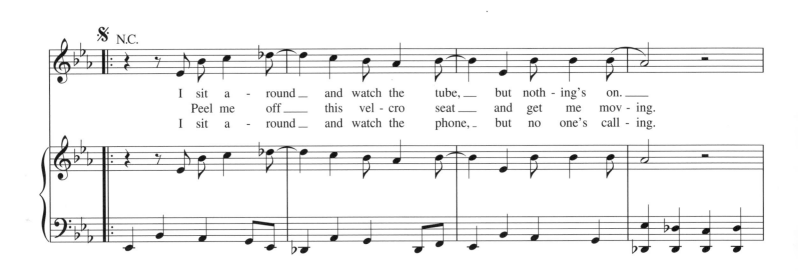

I sit a - round and watch the tube, but noth - ing's on.
Peel me off this vel - cro seat and get me mov - ing.
I sit a - round and watch the phone, but no one's call - ing.

I change the chan - nels for an hour or two.
I sure as hell can't do it by my - self.
Call me pa - thet - ic, call me what you will.

in - spi - - ra - - tion. ___

blind and ___ lone - li - ness ___ has to ___ suf - fice. ___ Bite my lip ___

MAYBE I'M AMAZED

Words and Music by
PAUL McCARTNEY

247

LOSING MY RELIGION

Words and Music by BILL BERRY, Peter Buck,
MIKE MILLS and MICHAEL STIPE

LOVE SHACK

Words and Music by CATHERINE E. PIERSON, FREDERICK W. SCHNEIDER,
KEITH J. STRICKLAND and CYNTHIA L. WILSON

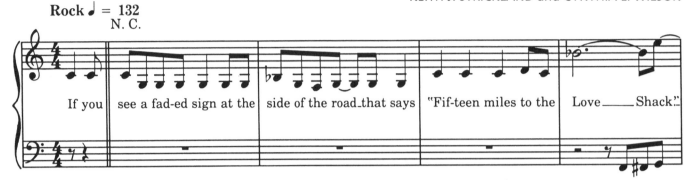

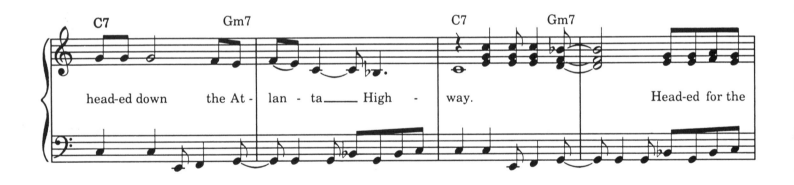

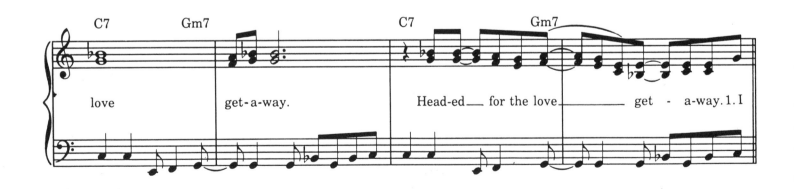

Verse 1, 3, & 6:

got me a car__ it's as | big as a whale__and we're head | - in' on down to the Love Shack. | I

got me a Chrys-ler, it | seats a-bout twen-ty. So | *hur-ry up and bring your* | *juke box mon-ey.* The

Chorus:

Love Shack__ is a | lit-tle old place where | we__ can get__ to - geth - er.__

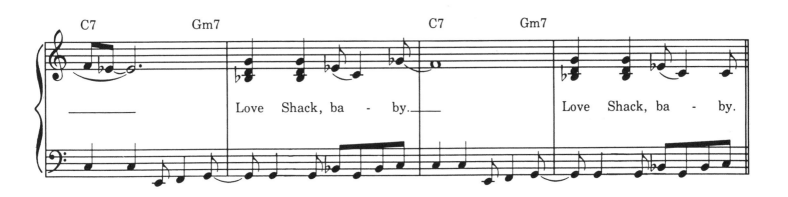

__ | Love Shack, ba - by.__ | Love Shack, ba - by.

On the door.— Your what? Tin ___ roof

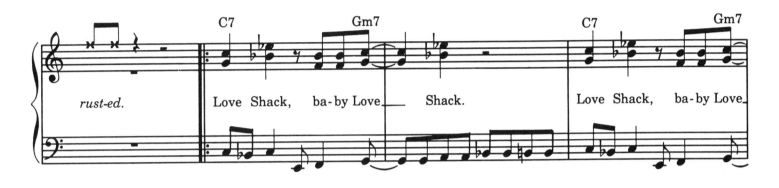

rust-ed. Love Shack, ba-by Love.___ Shack. Love Shack, ba-by Love.

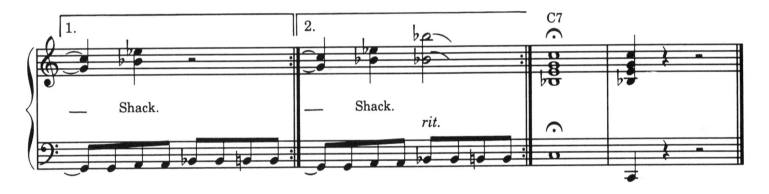

___ Shack. ___ Shack. rit.

Verse 3:
Glitter on the mattress, glitter on the highway.
Glitter on the front porch, glitter on the hallway.

Verse 4:
Huggin' and a kissin', dancin' and a lovin'.
Wearin' next to nothin' 'cause it's hot as an oven.
The whole shack shimmies, the whole shack shimmies,
The whole shack shimmies when everybody's movin'
Around and around and around and around.

Verse 6:
Hop in my Chrysler, it's as big as a whale,
And it's about to set sail.
I got me a car, it seats about twenty.
So hurry up and bring your juke box money.

MISS YOU

Words and Music by MICK JAGGER
and KEITH RICHARDS

(spoken) I've been

walk - ing Cen - tral Park,___ sing - ing af - ter dark,__ Peo - ple think I'm__ cra -

- zy, I've been stum - bling on my feet__ shuf - fling thro' the street__ ask - ing

peo - ple, "What's the mat - ter with you Jim boy?" Some - times

MMM BOP

Words and Music by ISAAC HANSON,
TAYLOR HANSON and ZAC HANSON

MY GENERATION

Words and Music by
PETER TOWNSHEND

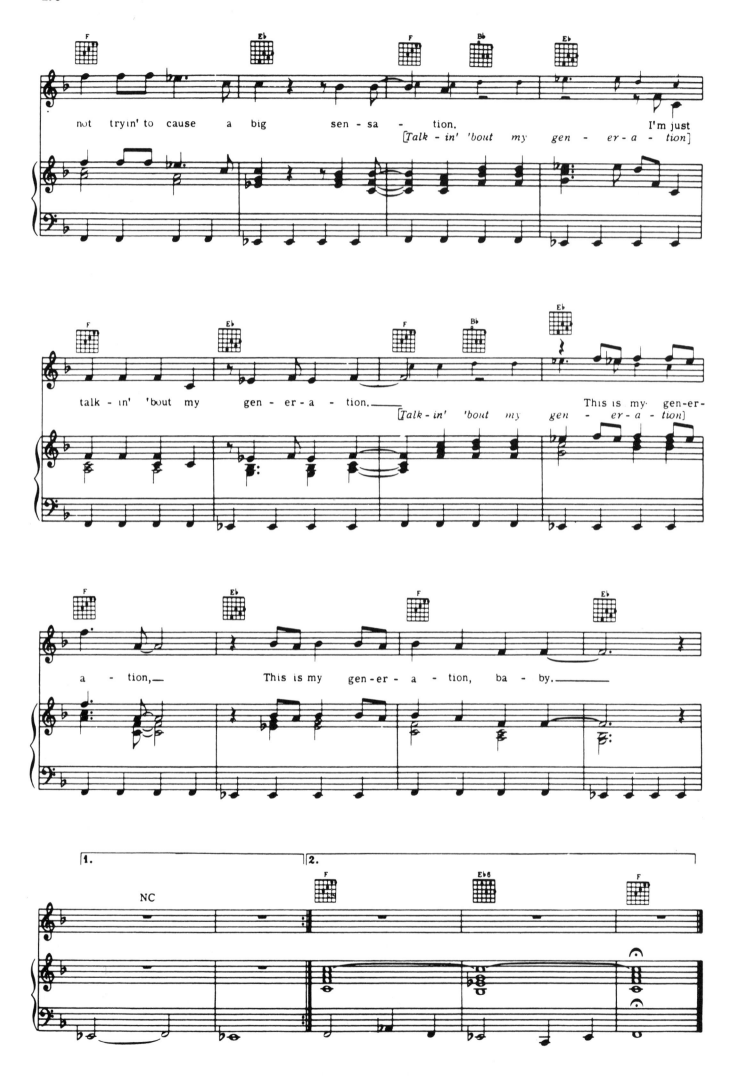

NASTY

Words and Music by JAMES HARRIS III,
TERRY LEWIS and JANET JACKSON

Oh, you nas-ty boys. Nas-ty, nas-ty boys,— give me your nas-ty groove.—

Oh, you nas-ty boys. Nas-ty, nas-ty boys,— let me

see your nas-ty bod-y move.—

Oh, you nas-ty boys.

Spoken: I could learn— to like

this.

Lis - ten up. *Sung:* I'm not a prude. ___ I

just want some re - spect. ___ So close the door ___ if you want me to ___ re - spond. ___

'Cause pri - va - cy ___ is my mid - dle name, my

last name is con - trol. ___ *Spoken:* No, my first name ain't Ba - by, it's

Who's that in that nas - ty car? __ (Nas - ty boys.) __

Who's that eat - in' that nas - ty food? __ (Nas - ty boys.) __

Who's jam-min' to my nas - ty groove? __ (Nas - ty boys.) __ La-dies? *Sung:* Nas - ty _____ boys

don't mean a thing. __ Oh, you nas - ty boys.

MY NAME IS

Words and Music by
LABI SIFFRE

Moderately slow
Chorus

Hi, my name is... What? My name is... Who? My name is Slim Shad - y.

Hi, my name is... Huh? My name is... What? My name is Slim Shad - y.

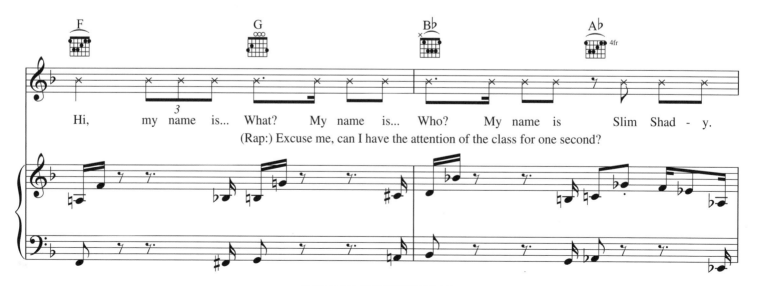

Hi, my name is... What? My name is... Who? My name is Slim Shad - y.

(Rap:) Excuse me, can I have the attention of the class for one second?

Chorus

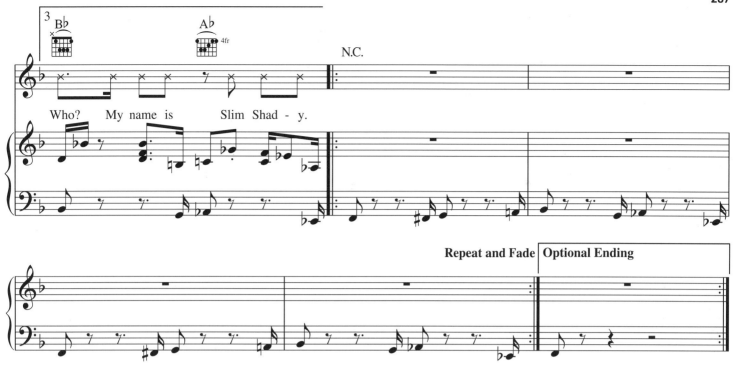

Who? My name is Slim Shad - y.

Repeat and Fade | **Optional Ending**

Rap Lyrics

1. Hi, kids. Do you like Primus? (yeah, yeah!)
   Wanna see me stick nine-inch nails
   Through each one of my eyelids? (Uh-huh!)
   Wanna copy me and do exactly like I did?
   Try 'cid and get messed up worse than my life is?
   My brain's dead weight.
   I'm tryin' to get my head straight,
   But I can't figure out which Spice Girl I wanna impregnate.
   And Dr. Dre said, "Slim Shady, you a bass head." (Uh-uh!)
   "Then why's your face red? Man, you're wasted!"
   Well, since age twelve, I felt like a caged elf
   Who stayed to himself in one space chasing his tail.
   Got ticked off and ripped Pamela Lee's lips off,
   Kissed 'em and said,
   "I ain't know silicone was supposed to be this soft."
   I'm about to pass out and crash and fall on the grass,
   Faster than a fat man who sat down too fast.
   Come here, lady.
   "Shady, wait a minute. That's my girl, dog."
   I don't give a damn,
   Dre sent me to tick the world off.
   Chorus

2. My English teacher wanted to flunk me in junior high.
   Thanks a lot - next semester I'll be thirty-five.
   I smacked him in his face with an eraser,
   Chased him with a stapler,
   And told him to change the grade on the paper.
   Walked in a strip club, had my jacket zipped up.
   Served the bartender and walked out with the tip cup.
   Extra-terrestrial runnin' over pedestrians in a space ship
   While they're screaming at me, "Let's just be friends!"
   Ninety-nine percent of my life I was lied to.
   I just found out my mom does more dope than I do.
   I told her I'd grow up to be a famous rapper,
   Make a record about doin' drugs and name it after her.
   You know you blew up when the women rush the stands
   And try to touch your hands like some screamin' Usher fans.
   This guy at White Castle asked for my autograph.
   So I signed it, "Dear Dave, Thanks for the support, *******!"
   Chorus

3. Stop the tape. This kid needs to be locked away! (Get him!)
   Dr. Dre, don't just stand there, operate!
   I'm not ready to leave, it's too scary to die.
   I'd rather be carried inside the cemetery and buried alive.
   Am I comin' or goin'? I can barely decide.
   I just drank a fifth of Coolade; dare me to drive? (Go ahead.)
   All my life I was very deprived.
   I ain't had a woman in years,
   And my palms are too hairy to hide.
   Clothes ripped like the Incredible Hulk.
   I spit when I talk, I **** anything that walks.
   When I was little, I used to get so hungry I would throw fits.
   "How you gonna breast-feed me, Mom? You ain't got no tits."
   I lay awake and strap myself in the bed, with a bulletproof vest on,
   And tap myself in the head, till I'm steamin' mad.
   And by the way, when you see my dad,
   Ask him if he bought a porno mag to see my ad.
   Chorus

NO DIGGITY

**Words and Music by CHAUNCEY HANNIBAL,
EDWARD RILEY, WILLIAM STEWART,
RICHARD VICK, LYNISE WALTERS
and BILL WITHERS**

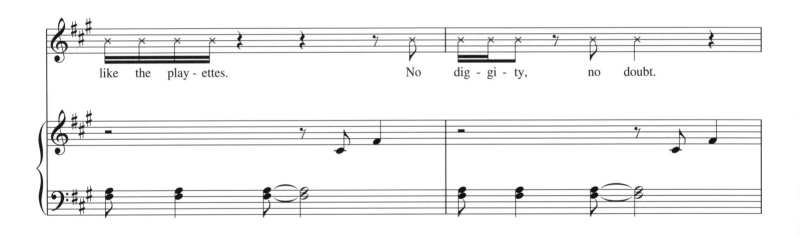

like it. No dig-gi-ty, no doubt. Yeah.

We out, we out. We out, we out.

(Spoken:) Blackstreet productions.

Rap I:

It's goin' down, fade to Blackstreet.
The homies got RB collab' creations.
Bump like acne, no doubt.
I put it down, never slouch.
As long as my credit could vouch,
A dog couldn't catch me staying out, and tell me,
Who could stop with Dre makin' moves,
Attractin' honeys like a magnet,
Giving them eargasms with my mellow accent
Still movin' his flavour
With the homies Blackstreet and Teddy,
The original rump shakers.

Verse 2:

She's got class and style,
Street knowledge by the pound.
Baby never act wild,
Very low key on the profile.
Catchin' villains is a no.
Let me tell you how it goes.
Curve's the word, spin's the verb,
Lovers it curves so freak what you heard.
Rollin' with the fatness,
You don't even know what the half is.
You got to pay to play
Just for shorty, bang bang, to look your way.
I like the way you work it,
Trump tight, all day, ev'ry day.
You're blowin' my mind, maybe in time,
Baby, I can get you in my ride.

Rap II:

Cuz, that's my peeps and we rows D,
Flyin' first class from New York City to Blackstreet.
What you know about me? Not a motherfucking thing.
Cartier wooded frames sported by my shorty.
As for me, icy gleam and pinky diamond ring.
We be's the baddest clique up on this scene.
Ain't you gettin' bored with these fake ass broads?
High shows and proves, no doubt, I be diggin' you.
So please excuse, if I come across rude.
That's just me and that's how a playette's got to be.
Stay kickin' game with a capital G.
Ask the peoples on my block, I'm as real as can be.
Word is born, fakin' moves never been my thing.
So, Teddy, pass the word to your nigga Chauncy,
I'll be sendin' a car, let's say around 3:30.
Queen Pen and Blackstreet, it's no diggity.

O.P.P.

Words and Music by ALPHONSO MIZELL,
FREDDIE PERREN, DENNIS LUSSIER, BERRY GORDY,
ANTHONY CRISS, KEIR GIST and VINCENT BROWN

Rap I: O.P.P.: how can I explain it?
I'll take you frame by frame it.
To have y'all jumpin', shall we singin' it.
O is for "other," P is for "people," scratchin' temple.
The last P, well, that's not that simple, huh.
It's sorta like a, well, another way to call a cat a kitten.
It's five letters that are missin' here.
You get it on occasion at the other party as a game,
An' it seems I gotta start the explainin'. Bust it.
You ever had a girl and met her on a nice hello?
You get her name and number, then you feelin' real mellow.
You get home, wait a day; she's what you wanna know about.
Then you call up and its her girlfriend's or her cousin's house.
It's not a fronter, F to the R to the O to the N to the T.
It's just her boyfriend's at her house. (Oh, that's what is scary.)
It's O.P.P. time, other people's what you get it.
There's no room for relationship, there's just room to hit it.
How many brothers out there know just what I'm gettin' at?
Who thinks it's wrong 'cause I was splittin' and co-hittin' at?
Well, if you do, that's O.P.P., and you're not down with it,
But if you don't, here's your membership.

Rap II: As for the ladies, O.P.P. means something gifted.
The first two letters are same, but the last is something different.
It's the longest, loveliest, lean—I call it the leanest.
It's another five letter word rhymin' with cleanest and meanest.
I won't get into that; I'll do it, uh, sorta properly.
I say the last P...hmm...stands for "property."
Now, lady, here comes a kiss, blow a kiss back to me.
Now, tell me, exactly,
Have you ever known a brother who had another, like a girl or wife?
And you just had to stop and just 'cause he look just as nice.
You looked at him, he looked at you, and you knew right away
That he had someone, but he was gonna be yours anyway.
You couldn't be seen with him, and honestly, you didn't care
'Cause in a room behind a door, no one but y'all are there.
When y'all are finished, y'all can leave, and only y'all would know,
And y'all could throw that skeleton bone right in the closet door.
Now, don't be shocked, 'cause if you're down, I want your hands up high.
Say, "O.P.P." (O.P.P), I like to say with pride.
Now when you do it, do it well, and make sure that it counts.
You're now down with a discount.

Rap III: This girl tried to O.P.P. me.
I had a girl, and she knew that, matter-of-fact, uh, my girl was partners
That had a fallout, disagreement, yeah, an argument.
She tried to do me so we did it in my apartment, bust it.
That wasn't the thing, it must have been the way she hit the ceiling,
'Cause after that, she kept on comin' back and catchin' feelings.
I said, "Let's go, my girl is comin', so you gotta leave."
She said, "Oh no, I love you, Treach."
I said, "Now, child, please,
You gots to leave, come grab your coat right now, you gotta go."
I said, "Now, look you to the stairs and to the stair window.
This was a thing, a little thing— you shouldn't have put your heart,
'Cause you know I was O.P.P, hell, from the very start."
Come on, come on, now let me tell you what it's all about.
When you get down, you can't go 'round runnin' off at the mouth.
That's rule number one in this O.P.P. establishment.
You keep your mouth shut and it won't get back to her or him.
Exciting, isn't it? A special kinda business.
Many of you will catch the same sorta O.P.P visit with
Him or her, for sure, are goin' to admit it.
When O.P.P comes, damn, skippy, I'm with it.

OH, PRETTY WOMAN

Words and Music by ROY ORBISON
and BILL DEES

Hey, O. K.

If that's the way it must be ___ O. K.

I guess I'll go on home, ___ it's late ___ There'll be to -

mor - row night but wait! What do I see? ___

ONE

Lyrics by BONO and THE EDGE
Music by U2

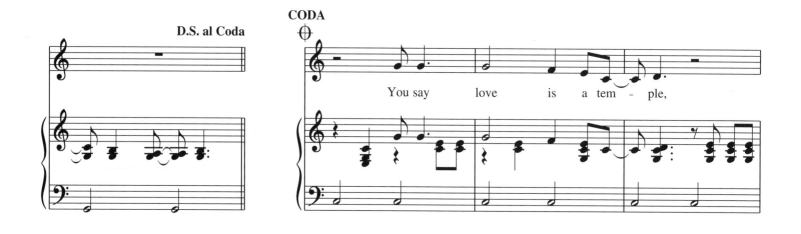

You say love is a tem - ple,

love a high-er law, ___ love is ___ a tem - ple,

ONE HEADLIGHT

Words and Music by
JAKOB DYLAN

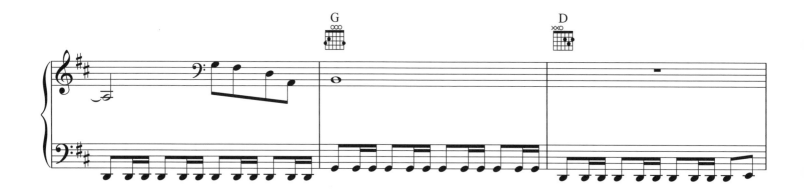

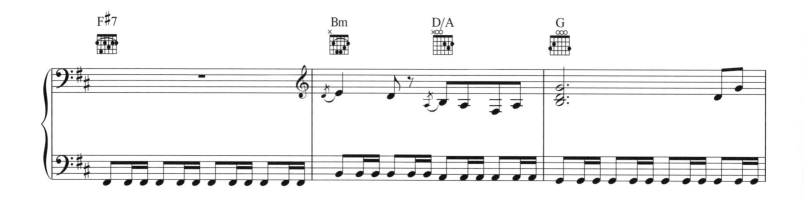

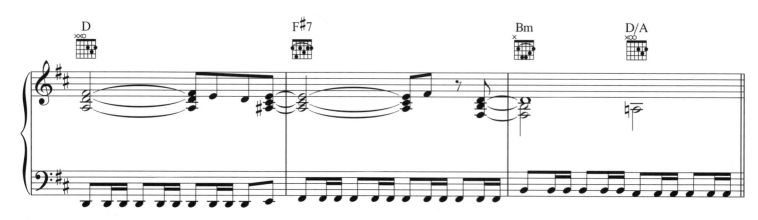

So long a - go, I don't re - mem - ber when, __ That's when they say I lost my on - ly
cold, it feels like In - de - pen - dence Day, __ and I can't __ break a - way from this pa -
cold, it feels just like a beat - up truck, __ I turn the en - gine but the en - gine does - n't

friend. Well, they said she died eas - y of a bro - ken heart dis - ease, as I
rade. But there's got to be an o - pen - ing __ some - where here in front of me, __
turn. Well, it smells of cheap __ wine and cig - a - rettes, this place is al - ways such a mess. Some

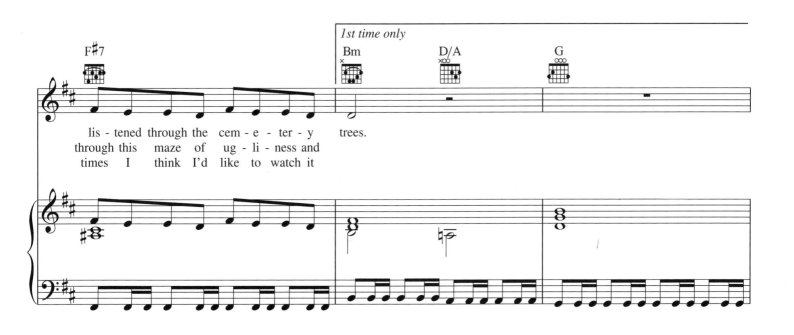

1st time only

lis - tened through the cem - e - ter - y trees.
through this maze of ug - li - ness and
times I think I'd like to watch it

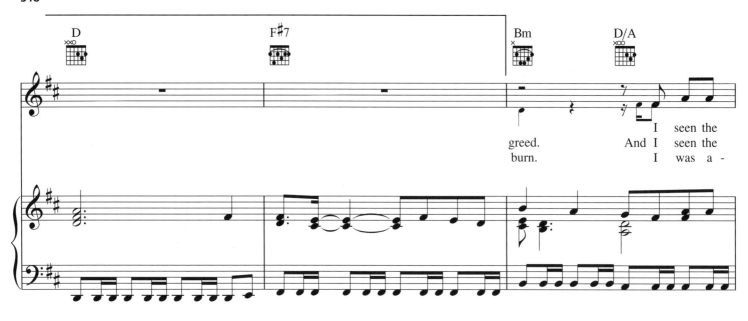

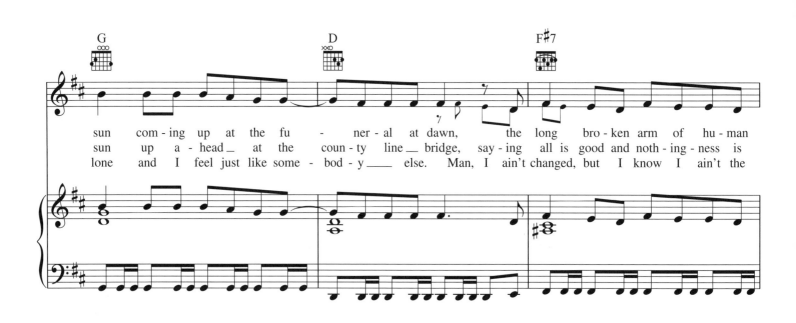

THE ONE I LOVE

Words and Music by BILL BERRY,
PETER BUCK, MIKE MILLS and MICHAEL STIPE

ONLY HAPPY WHEN IN RAINS

Words and Music by DUKE ERIKSON,
SHIRLEY ANN MANSON, STEVE MARKER
and BUTCH VIG

Original key: G♯ minor. This edition has been transposed down one half-step to be more playable.

PAPA DON'T PREACH

Words and Music by
BRIAN ELLIOT

OUR LIPS ARE SEALED

Words and Music by JANE WIEDLIN
and TERRY HALL

Original key: A major. This edition has been transposed down one half-step to be more playable.

PHOTOGRAPH

Words and Music by STEVE CLARK,
JOE ELLIOTT, ROBERT JOHN LANGE,
RICK SAVAGE and PETE WILLIS

PROUD MARY

Words and Music by
J.C. FOGERTY

Moderately

Left a good job in the cit-y, workin' for the man ev-'ry
Cleaned a lot of plates in Mem-phis, pumped a lot of 'pane down in
If you come down to the riv-er, bet you gon-na find some

night and day. And I nev-er lost one min-ute of sleep-in',
New Or-leans. But I nev-er saw the good side of the cit-y
peo-ple who live. You don't have to wor-ry 'cause you have no mon-ey.

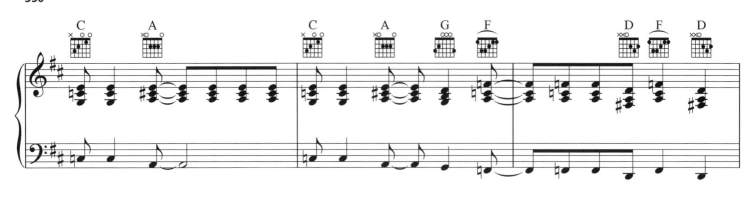

D.S. al Coda

RESPECT

Words and Music by
OTIS REDDING

(just a lit - tle bit.) I'm a-bout to give you all __ of my mon - ey

and all I'm ask - in' in re - turn, hon - ey, is to give me

my prop - ers when you get home, yeah, ba - by, when you get
(Just a just a just a just a just a just a just a just a)

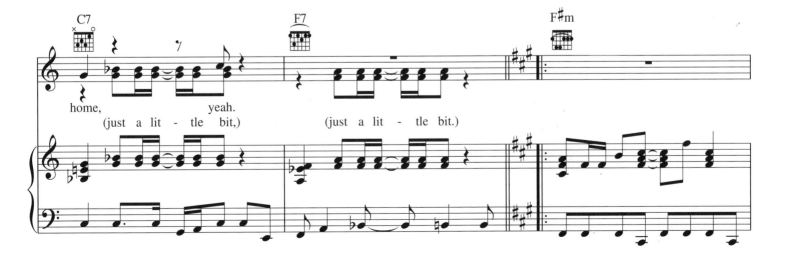

home, yeah.
(just a lit - tle bit,) (just a lit - tle bit.)

ROCK WITH YOU

Words and Music by
ROD TEMPERTON

This edition has been transposed up one half-step to be more playable.

D/F#
Cmaj9
lay back and groove
'cause we've got so far
G/A
Em7
F#m7
Gmaj7
with mine. You've got - ta feel that heat, and - a
to go. When you feel that heat and - a
Em7
F#m7
Gmaj7
G
A
we can ride the boog - ie,
we're gon - na ride the boog - ie,
share that beat of love.
Em9
I wan - na rock with you,
8vb

floor ___ there ain't no - bod - y there but

us. Girl, _____ when you

dance _____ there's a mag - ic that must be

love. _____

D.S. al Coda

CODA

SHE DRIVES ME CRAZY

Words and Music by DAVID STEELE
and ROLAND GIFT

SMELLS LIKE TEEN SPIRIT

Words and Music by KURT COBAIN,
CHRIS NOVOSELIC and DAVID GROHL

Load up ___ on guns, ___ bring ___ your friends. ___
I'm worse ___ at what ___ I ___ do best, ___
And I ___ for - get ___ just why ___ I ___ taste. ___

___ It's fun ___ to lose ___ and to ___ pre - tend. ___ She's o - ver - bored, ___
___ and for ___ this gift ___ I feel ___ blessed. ___ Our lit - tle trap ___
___ Oh, yeah, ___ I guess ___ it makes ___ me smile. ___ I found ___ it hard; ___

Ab5 Db5 F5 Bb5 Ab5 Db5
4fr
-g'rous. Here we are now; en-ter-tain us. I feel stu-
F5 Bb5 Ab5 Db5 F5 Bb5
-pid and con-ta-gious. Here we are now; en-ter-tain
Ab5 Db5 F5 Bb5 Ab5 Db5
To Coda
us. A mu-lat-to, an al-bi-no, a mos-qui-
F5 Bb5 Ab5 Db5 F5 E5 F5 Gb5
N.C.
-to, my li-bi-do. Yeah! Oy.

SMOOTH

Words by ROB THOMAS
Music by ROB THOMAS and ITAAL SHUR

STAYIN' ALIVE
from the Motion Picture SATURDAY NIGHT FEVER

Words and Music by BARRY GIBB,
MAURICE GIBB and ROBIN GIBB

SUPERSTITION

Words and Music by
STEVIE WONDER

Ooh,__ ver - y su - per - sti -

D.S. al Coda

Ver - y su - per - sti -

CODA

N.C.

E♭m

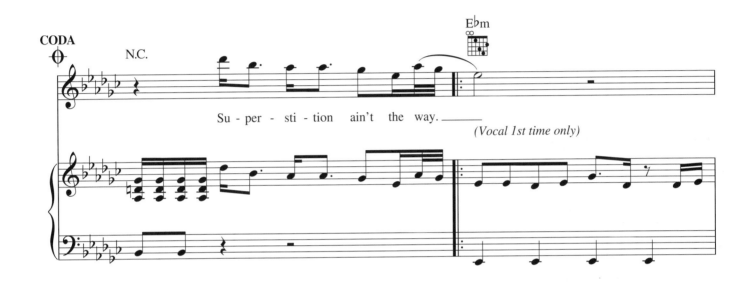

Su - per - sti - tion ain't the way. _____
(Vocal 1st time only)

Repeat and Fade

Optional Ending

SURRENDER

Words and Music by
RICK NIELSEN

Moderately

Mother told __ me, yes she told __ me,
Father says, __ "Your moth-er's right, __ she's

I'd meet girls __ like you. __
real-ly up __ on things." __

She al-so told __ me stay __
Be-fore we mar-ried Mom-

__ a-way, __ you'll nev-er know what you'll __ catch. __
-my served __ in the WACs __ in the Phil-ip-pines. __

Now

SWEET CHILD O' MINE

Words and Music by W. AXL ROSE, SLASH, IZZY STRADLIN',
DUFF McKAGAN and STEVEN ADLER

*Recorded a half step lower.

1. She's got a smile___ that it seems to me___ re - minds___ me of child - hood
2. *See additional lyrics*

mem - o - ries, ___ where ev - 'ry - thing___ was as fresh___

Play 4 times

Additional Lyrics

2. She's got eyes of the bluest skies, as if they thought of rain.
   I hate to look into those eyes and see an ounce of pain.
   Her hair reminds me of a warm safe place where as a child I'd hide,
   And pray for the thunder and the rain to quietly pass me by. *(To Chorus)*

TAINTED LOVE

Words and Music by
ED COBB

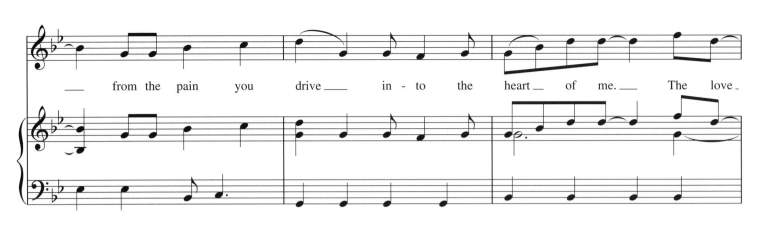

from the pain you drive ___ in-to the heart ___ of me. ___ The love ___

___ we share ___ seems to go no - where, ___ and I've

lost my light, ___ for I toss and turn. ___ I can't sleep at night.

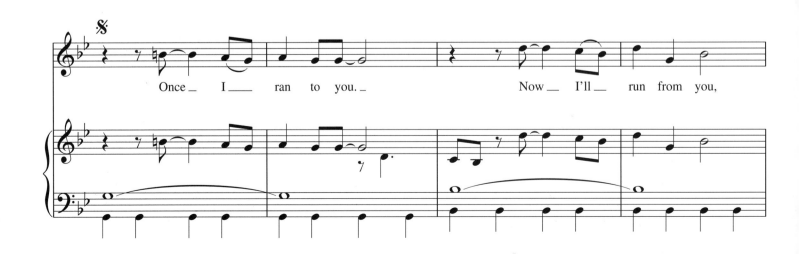

Once ___ I ___ ran to you. ___ Now ___ I'll ___ run from you,

this taint - ed love ___ you've giv - en. I give you all ___ a boy ___

To Coda ⊕

___ could give ___ you. Take my tears and that's not liv - ing.

Oh taint - ed love, ___ taint - ed love. ___

Now I know ___ I've got to run a - way. ___ I've got to

get a - way.____ You don't real - ly want____ it an - y -
more from me.____ To make____ things right____ you need some - one____
____ to hold you tight.____ And you'll think love is to pray.____

D.S. al Coda

____ But I'm sor - ry I____ don't pray that way.

TANGLED UP IN BLUE

Words and Music by
BOB DYLAN

1. Ear-ly one morn-in' the sun __ was shin-in', I was lay-in' in bed, __
2. She __ was mar-ried when we __ first met, soon to be __ di-vorced. __
3. I had a job in the great __ North woods, work-in' as a cook for a spell. __ But I
4.-7. *(See additional lyrics)*
8. *Instrumental*

won - d'rin' if __ she's changed at all, __ if her hair was __ still red. __
I helped her out of a jam, I guess, __ but I used a lit - tle too much force. __ We
nev - er did like __ it all that much __ and one day the axe just fell. __ So I

Tang - led up in blue. ____
tang - led up in blue. ____

Additional Lyrics

4. She was working in topless place
   And I stopped in for a beer.
   I just kept looking at the side of her face
   In the spotlight so clear.
   And later on when the crowd thinned out
   I was just about to do the same.
   She was standing there in back of my chair,
   Said to me, "Don't I know your name?"
   I muttered something underneath my breath.
   She studied the lines on my face.
   I must admit I felt a little uneasy
   When she bent down to tie the laces of my shoe,
   Tangled up in blue.

5. She lit a burner on the stove
   And offered me a pipe.
   "I thought you'd never say hello," she said.
   "You look like the silent type."
   Then she opened up a book of poems
   And handed it to me,
   Written by an Italian poet
   From the thirteenth century.
   And every one of them words rang true
   And glowed like burning coal,
   Pourin' off of every page
   Like it was written in my soul,
   From me to you,
   Tangled up in blue.

6. I lived with them on Montague Street
   In a basement down the stairs.
   There was music in the cafes at night
   And revolution in the air.
   Then he started in the dealing in slaves
   And something inside of him died.
   She had to sell everything she owned
   And froze up inside.
   And when finally the bottom finally fell out
   I became withdrawn.
   The only thing I knew how to do
   Was to keep on keeping on,
   Like a bird that flew
   Tangled up in blue.

7. So now I'm going back again.
   I got to get to her somehow.
   All the people we used to know,
   They're an illusion to me now.
   Some are mathematicians,
   Some are carpenter's wives.
   Don't know how it all got started,
   I don't know what they do with their lives.
   But me, I'm still on the road
   Headin' for another joint.
   We always did feel the same,
   We just saw it from a different point of view,
   Tangled up in blue.

TEARS IN HEAVEN

Words and Music by ERIC CLAPTON
and WILL JENNINGS

Would you know my name _____
Would you hold my hand _____
Would you know my name _____

if I saw you in heav - en?
if I I saw you in heav - en?
if I saw you in heav - en?

Would it be the same _____
Would you help me stand _____
Would you be the same _____

Be - yond the door _____ there's peace, I'm sure, _

and I know ___ there'll be no more ___ tears in heav-

en.

UNDER THE BRIDGE

Words and Music by ANTHONY KIEDIS, FLEA,
JOHN FRUSCIANTE and CHAD SMITH

Some-times I feel ___ like I
drive on her streets ___ 'cause
hard to be - lieve ___ that there's

don't have a part - ner.
she's my com - pan - ion.   I
no - bod - y out ___ there.   It's

Some - times I feel ___ like
walk through her hills 'cause she
hard to be - lieve ___ that

TIME AFTER TIME

Words and Music by CYNDI LAUPER
and ROB HYMAN

TINY DANCER

Words and Music by ELTON JOHN
and BERNIE TAUPIN

And now ___ she's in me, ___ al - ways ___ with me, ___
Look - ing on, _____ she sings the ___ songs. _____

ti - ny danc - er in my hand. _____
The word she ___ knows, the tune she hums. _____

But oh how it feels ___ so real ___

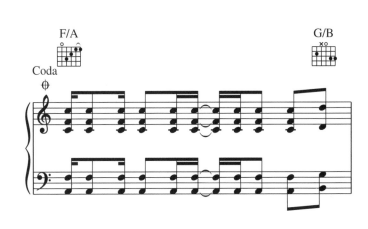

*D.S. al Coda

Coda

**On Verse repeat, take 2nd ending;
on Chorus repeat, take both endings.*

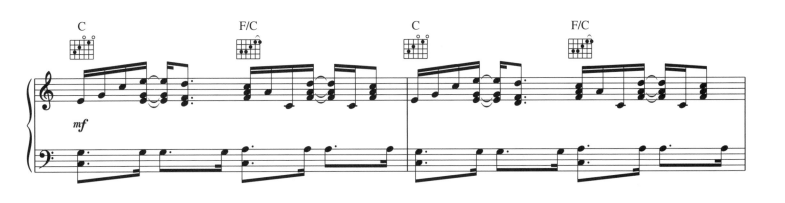

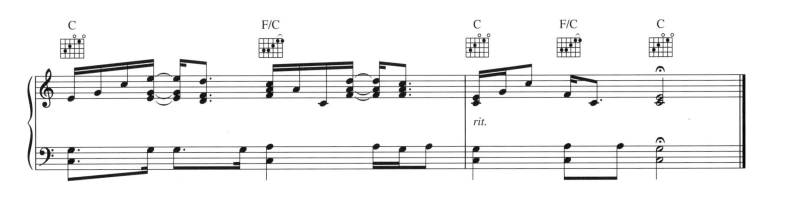

THE TRACKS OF MY TEARS

Words and Music by WILLIAM "SMOKEY" ROBINSON,
WARREN MOORE and MARVIN TARPLIN

VOGUE

Words and Music by MADONNA CICCONE
and SHEP PETTIBONE

Vogue, (Vogue.) Beau-ty's where you find it. (Go —

— with the flow. —) *Spoken: Greta Garbo and Monroe, Deitrich and DiMaggio,*

Marlon Brando, Jimmy Dean, *on the cover of a magazine.* *Grace Kelly, Harlow, Jean;*

picture of a beauty queen. *Gene Kelly, Fred Astaire,* *Ginger Rodgers dance on air.*

WATERFALLS

Words and Music by MARQUEZE ETHERIDGE,
LISA NICOLE LOPES, RICO R. WADE,
PAT BROWN and RAMON MURRAY

Relaxed R&B shuffle

A lone-ly moth-er gaz-ing out of her win-dow star-ing
Lit-tle pre-cious has a nat-'ral ob-ses-sion for temp-

452

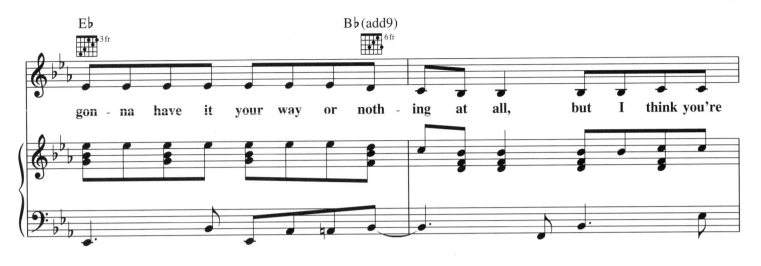

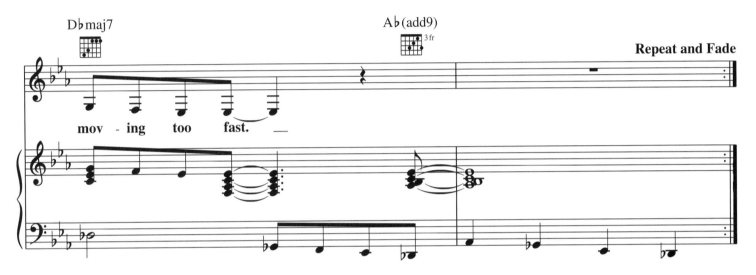

Additional Lyrics

Rap: **I seen a rainbow yesterday**
But too many storms have come and gone
Leavin' a trace of not one God-given ray
Is it because my life is ten shades of gray
I pray all ten fade away
Seldom praise Him for the sunny days
And like His promise is true
Only my faith can undo
The many chances I blew
To bring my life to anew
Clear blue and unconditional skies
Have dried the tears from my eyes
No more lonely cries
My only bleedin' hope
Is for the folk who can't cope
Wit such an endurin' pain
That it keeps 'em in the pourin' rain
Who's to blame
For tootin' caine in your own vein
What a shame
You shoot and aim for someone else's brain
You claim the insane
And name this day in time
For fallin' prey to crime
I say the system got you victim to your own mind
Dreams are hopeless aspirations
In hopes of comin' true
Believe in yourself
The rest is up to me and you

WHAT'S GOING ON

Words and Music by MARVIN GAYE,
AL CLEVELAND and RENALDO BENSON

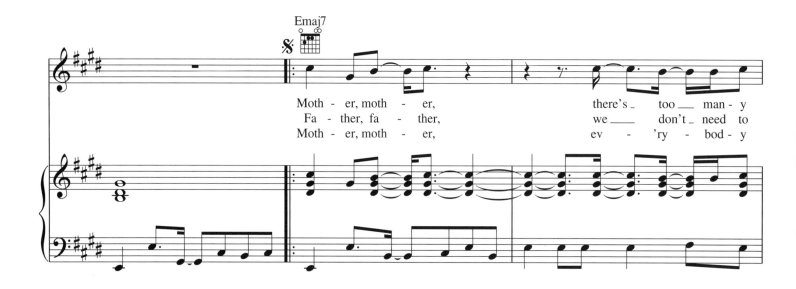

Moth - er, moth - er,   there's _ too _ man - y
Fa - ther, fa - ther,   we _ don't _ need to
Moth - er, moth - er,   ev - 'ry - bod - y

of you cry - ing.   Broth - er, broth - er, broth - er,
es - ca - late. _____   You see, _ war is not _ the an - swer,
thinks we're wrong. ___   Ah, but _ who are they _ to judge _ us

F#m7   F#m7/B

pun - ish me   with ___ bru - tal - i - ty.

F#m7   F#m7/B

Talk to me   so you can see,   oh, what's

Emaj7   C#m7   4fr

go - ing on, ___   what's go - ing on, ___   yeah, what's

To Coda ⊕

Emaj7   C#m7   4fr

go - ing on, ___   oh, what's go - ing on. ___   Ah, ___ ah, ah, ___

WHERE DID OUR LOVE GO

Words and Music by BRIAN HOLLAND,
LAMONT DOZIER and EDWARD HOLLAND

(1.,3.) Ba - by, ba - by, ba - by, don't leave me.
(2.) Ba - by, ba - by, where _ did our love go?

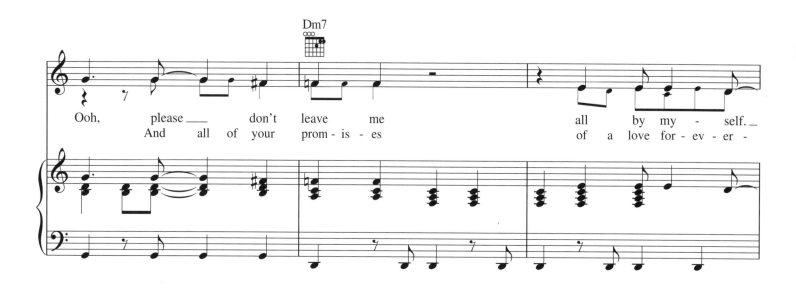

Ooh, please _ don't leave me all by my - self. _
And all of your prom - is - es of a love for - ev - er -

_ more!} I've _ got this burn - ing, burn - ing,

Don't you want me no more? (ba - by ba - by) Ooh, ba - by.

D.C. al Coda

CODA

Be - fore__ you won my heart, (ba - by ba - by)

WONDERWALL

Words and Music by
NOEL GALLAGHER

YESTERDAY

Words and Music by JOHN LENNON
and PAUL McCARTNEY

Moderately, with expression

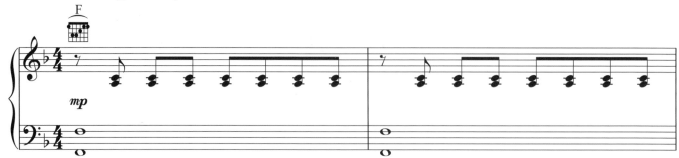

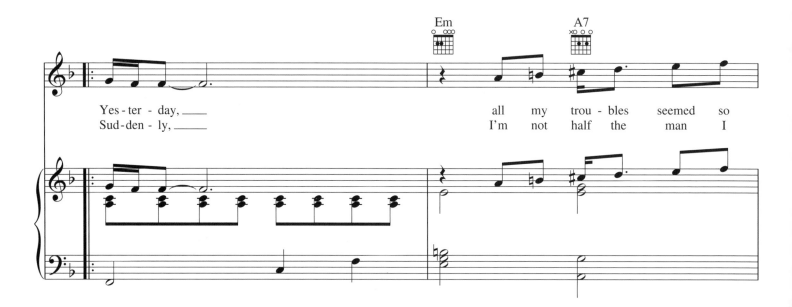

Yes - ter - day, ___ all my trou - bles seemed so
Sud - den - ly, ___ I'm not half the man I

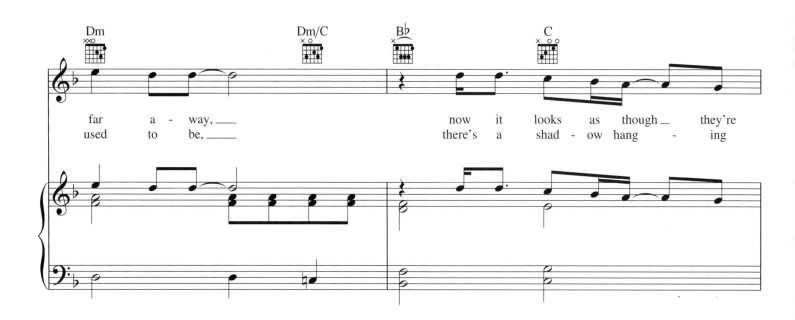

far a - way, ___ now it looks as though ___ they're
used to be, ___ there's a shad - ow hang - ing

YOU ARE THE SUNSHINE OF MY LIFE

Words and Music by
STEVIE WONDER

YOU OUGHTA KNOW

Lyrics by ALANIS MORISSETTE
Music by ALANIS MORISSETTE
and GLEN BALLARD

YOU SHOOK ME ALL NIGHT LONG

Words and Music by ANGUS YOUNG,
MALCOLM YOUNG and BRIAN JOHNSON

* Vocal written at pitch.

G C G C G D5 G
fast ma - chine; she kept the mo - tor clean. She was the best damn wom - an that I've
dou - ble time on the se - duc - tion line she was one of a kind, she's just
D5 G D5 G C G C G D5
ev - er seen. She had the sight - less eyes tell - in' men no lies and
mine, all mine. Want - ed no ap - plause just an - oth - er cause, Made a
G D5 G D5 G C
knock - in' me out with those A - mer - i - can thighs. Tak - in' more than her share, had me
meal out of me and come back for more. Had to cool me down to take an -
G C G D5 G D5 G D5
fight - in' for air. She told me to come, but I was al - read - y there. 'Cause the
- oth - er round. Now I'm back in the ring to take an - oth - er swing. That the
5fr

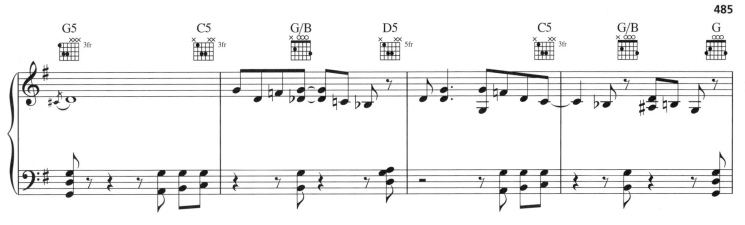

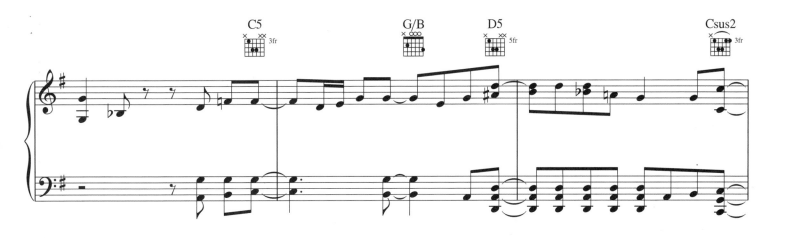

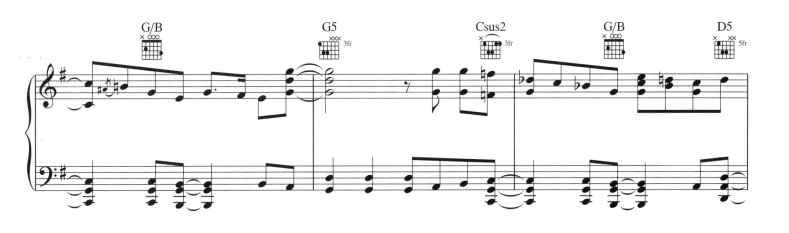

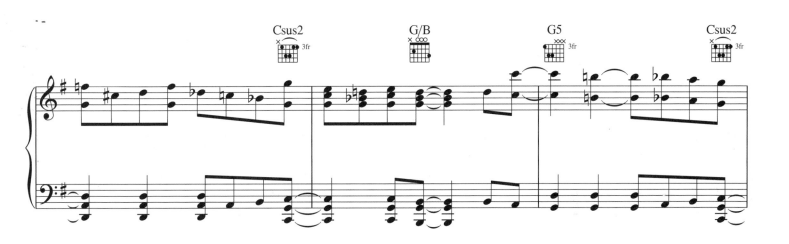

YOUR SONG

Words and Music by ELTON JOHN
and BERNIE TAUPIN

Slow, but with a beat

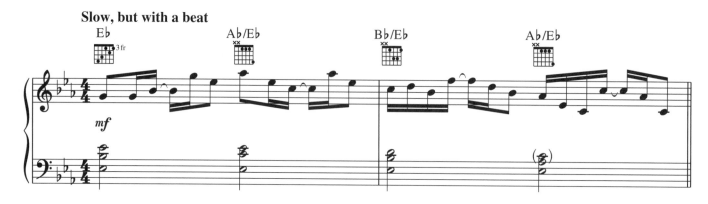

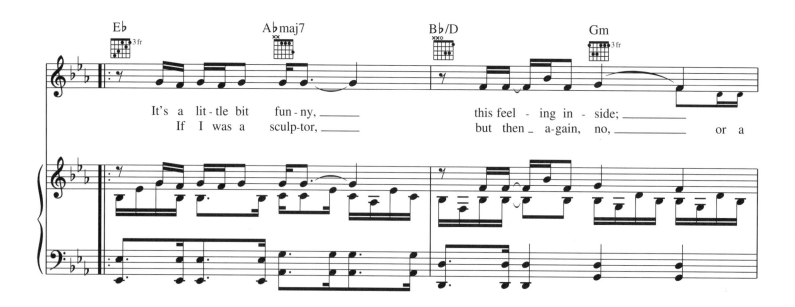

It's a lit-tle bit fun-ny, _____ this feel-ing in-side; _____
If I was a sculp-tor, _____ but then _ a-gain, no, _____ or a

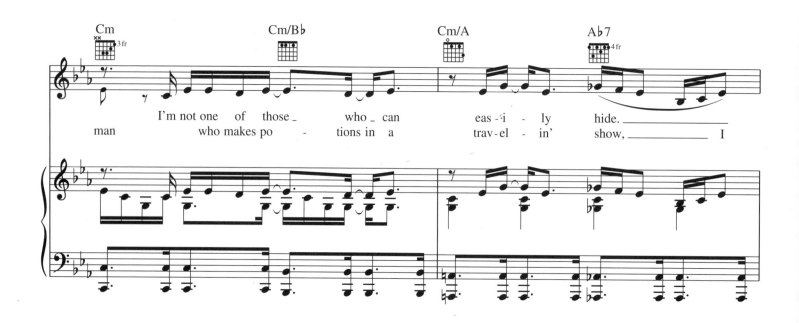

I'm not one of those _ who _ can eas-i-ly hide. _____
man who makes po - tions in a trav-el-in' show, _____ I